ST CYPRIAN OF CARTHAGE

On the Church: Select Treatises

T0326957

ST VLADIMIR'S SEMINARY PRESS
Popular Patristics Series
Number 32

The Popular Patristics Series published by St Vladimir's Seminary Press provides readable and accurate translations of a wide
range of early Christian literature to a wide audience—students
of Christian history to lay Christians reading for spiritual benefit.
Recognized scholars in their fields provide short but comprehensive and clear introductions to the material. The texts include
classics of Christian literature, thematic volumes, collections of
homilies, letters on spiritual counsel, and poetical works from a
variety of geographical contexts and historical backgrounds. The
mission of the series is to mine the riches of the early Church and
to make these treasures available to all.

Series Editor
BOGDAN BUCUR

Associate Editor
IGNATIUS GREEN

* * *

Series Editor
1999–2020
JOHN BEHR

ST CYPRIAN OF CARTHAGE

On the Church
Select Treatises

Translation with Introduction and
Commentary by

ALLEN BRENT

ST VLADIMIR'S SEMINARY PRESS
CRESTWOOD, NEW YORK
2006

Library of Congress Cataloging-in-Publication Data

Cyprian, Saint, Bishop of Carthage.
  [Treatises. English. Selections]
  On the church : select treatises / St. Cyprian of Carthage ; translation with
introduction and commentary by Allen Brent.
        p. cm. — (St. Vladimir's Seminary Press "popular patristics" series ; no. 32)
        Includes bibliographical references (p.   ).
        ISBN–13: 978–0–88141–312–0 (alk. paper)
        ISBN–10: 0–88141–312–7 (alk. paper)
        1. Church discipline—History—Early church, ca. 30–600. 2. Church—
Unity. 3. Cyprian, Saint, Bishop of Carthage. I. Brent, Allen. II. Title. III. Series.

  BR65.C82E52 2006
  262'.013—dc22

                                                            2006017889

COPYRIGHT © 2006
ST VLADIMIR'S SEMINARY PRESS
575 Scarsdale Rd, Crestwood, NY 10707
1-800-204-2665
www.svspress.com

ISBN 0–88141–312–7
ISBN 978–088141–312–0
ISSN 1555–5755

PRINTED IN THE UNITED STATES OF AMERICA

Caroline Penrose Hammond Bammel, F.B.A.
In piam memoriam

Contents

References are in accordance with the abbreviations in
The SBL Handbook of Style (Peabody, MA: Hendrickson, 1999).

*Means that the work is not included in this present translation.

Psalms are cited according to the Vulgate/LXX numeration.

Preface

These translations with their introductions and notes are the product of a continuing research project begun at the British School at Rome in 1999, supported then by a Grant in Aid of Research by the Leverhulme Trust. My work has been concerned with the interface between the development of church order and Christian theology and Graeco Roman culture and history.

Cyprian was the great publicist who argued his theory of church unity with such success that it achieved almost universal acceptance before the European Reformation. To be a member of the Church that is the body of Christ you needed to be in communion with a priest who was in communion with a bishop who in turn was in communion with all other bishops in the world. But how could you tell or decide? And on what kind of issue would it be right for dioceses to break off communion with each other, or to threaten to do so?

Were there not other kinds of self-authenticating ministries, like those of martyrs and confessors who had suffered for the Faith? And did the Church not need, and in what form, a universal bishop who could guarantee the integrity of the network of bishops? These were the questions with which Cyprian wrestled and to which he sought to give answers in his selected works translated in this book and in its companion volume, *On the Church: Select Letters*, SVS Popular Patristics Series, Number 33. They are questions that continue to be asked in the contemporary Church.

The appearance of a new work of this nature is timely given the stalling of the process of ecumenical reconciliation, for which there seemed so great hopes in the 60s and 70s of the last century.

In Cyprian's work we have the classical statement of church order, based upon the theology of a bishop presiding over a diocese but needing to remain in communion with the episcopal college throughout the world. It is a work that continues to raise issues that are pertinent to the modern church.

These two volumes are presented in the hope that they will assist our understanding of the historical and cultural development of this historical order of Christendom and the form in which it may be continued in those churches that claim to continue the historic episcopate (Orthodox, Roman and Anglican), and in others who seek mutual understanding and reconciliation with it.

ALLEN BRENT
St Edmund's College, Cambridge

Introduction

§1 The Life of Cyprian

Little is known of the early life of Cyprian. We possess a *Life of Cyprian* by the deacon Pontius, which is in reality rather an apologetic defense of his subject against critics within the Church. These critics distrusted his meteoric rise from converted layman to bishop, and would not accept Cyprian's flight into hiding during persecution as anything but cowardice.[1] Pontius ignores his pagan life prior to his conversion, but focuses upon his actions as a bishop and the details of his martyrdom. Subsequent to his death in AD 258, such an apology would have had a point in view of his controversy with Pope Stephen over the issue of rebaptizing schismatics and heretics.[2] We have in addition the *Consular Acts (Acta Proconsularia) of Carthage,* also with an account of his martyrdom, which Pontius appears to have utilized.[3] We also possess some statements by Jerome and Augustine.[4]

Thacius Caecilius Cyprianus may have been born around AD 202, and became a teacher of rhetoric following the relevant course of pagan, classical education. His ancestral country estate (*horti*) was in his birthplace, Carthage. Thus he owed both wealth and education to his family and not to a patron. Shadows of his pagan career seem to have left their traces on his treatises *Ad Donatum* and *Ad*

---

[1] See *Ep.* 81.

[2] See *Ep.*73 and 75, and **Ep.* 74.

[3] For a discussion of the problems of the biography, see M. Sage, *Cyprian,* Patristics Monographs Series 1 (Philadelphia, PA: Philadelphia Patristic Foundation, 1975), 385–94.

[4] Jerome *Vir. ill.* 53; *Ep.* 84.2; Augustine *Serm.* 312.4.

Demetrianum, for which see the notes and commentary accompanying the present translations of these works.

Following his conversion, Cyprian was baptised into the Catholic Church at the time of the Easter Vigil, around AD 246. He took the name of his Christian teacher, the presbyter Caecilian.[5] Along with that experience went a commitment to celibacy that also characterized membership of many pagan philosophical schools.[6] In *Donatus* we will read his own description of his divine illumination in his "Second Birth." He turned from what he characterizes as a corrupt and hypocritical society of Roman, North Africa, on its way to cosmic ruin in the collapsing world society of the mid-third century.[7] His reflections there on the law courts in the Forum seem supportive of Jerome's description of his fame as a *rhetor*, who practiced and taught oratory generally, and perhaps even specifically as an *aduocatus* practicing law.[8] Around 248, following the death of another Donatus, bishop of Carthage, Cyprian was apparently with some reluctance elected bishop of Carthage by the clergy and people.

Cyprian was a neophyte, or newly baptised. As such he was bypassing the minor orders such as reader, acolyte, and doorkeeper, and even the diaconate itself, and succeeding with unseemly haste to the episcopate. He showed the generosity with his wealth to the Church that was characteristic of those of curial or magisterial rank towards their clients and supporters.[9] It may well have been that the "old guard" of five presbyters who led the opposition resented the way in which a man of wealth, influence, and education came to the episcopate. To them Cyprian might have seemed too much like a secular, Roman *patronus* whose links of charity with his subservient

---

[5] Pontius *Vita* 4.
[6] Pontius *Vita* 2.4–5.
[7] Cyprian *Don.* 4.
[8] Jerome *Vir. ill.* 67.53. See also G. W. Clarke, "The Secular Profession of St Cyprian of Carthage," *Latomus* 24 (1965): 633–638.
[9] Pontius *Vita* 2.7.

clients lead to influence and votes for the magistracies that he chose to pursue.[10]

In AD 249 Decius Trajan became emperor of an empire that had been almost permanently in a state of revolt for thirteen years, with the frontiers threatened externally by the Goths in the West and Persia to the East, while rival claimants for the empire clashed with each other in civil war. Famine and pestilence were adding to a political crisis reflected in a widespread feeling of hopelessness in the face of decline. Decius gave himself the name of Trajan when he made his entrance into Rome in triumph in the last months of 249. As such he associated himself with the image of Trajan in contemporary historiography as the most enlightened of Emperors, having been commemorated as such in Pliny's *Panegyricus*, who had reigned over an empire in victorious peace. His edict, that all imperial subjects should sacrifice to the gods of the Roman state, was promulgated in late 249–250. Cyprian went into hiding, citing in justification Mt 10.33, from which place he administered his Church.[11] Later, we shall consider the divisions caused by the question of how to deal with those Christians who sacrificed (§2.1). Fabian, bishop of Rome was martyred, and Dionysius, bishop of Alexandria, went, like Cyprian, into hiding. Cornelius was to succeed Fabian in an election that was disputed after an interregnum in which Novatian appeared as a rival bishop.

In June 251, following the death both of the emperor Decius and his son, Trebonius Gallus became emperor and the policy of general

---

[10]Pontius *Vita* 5.6; cf. Cyprian *Ep.* 59.9. Bobertz has argued convincingly that it was the social discourse of the client-patron relationship with his original electors that enabled Cyprian to rebuild his authority in the chaotic situation that he found within the Carthaginian Church on his return from hiding; see C. A. Bobertz, *Cyprian of Carthage as Patron: A Social and Historical Study of the Role of Bishop in the Ancient Christian Community of North Africa* (Ann Arbor, MI: UMI, 1993); idem, "Patronage Networks and the Study of Ancient Christianity," in StPatr 24 (1991): 20–27; idem, "Patronal Letters of Commendation: Cyprian's *Epistulae* 38–40," StPatr 31 (1995): 252–59.

[11]Cyprian *Ep.* 5.2 and 7.2; cf. *Laps.* 10. For criticisms of Cyprian see *Ep.* 8.

persecution appears to have ceased. Councils could now take place in Carthage (23 March 251) and in Rome (251) on the divisive question over the appropriate treatment of the lapsed or fallen. It was in connection with these divisions that, at this time, Cyprian wrote both his work *On the Fallen (De lapsis)*, and *The Unity of the Catholic Church (De catholicae ecclesiae unitate)*.

A plague followed, the experiences of which occasioned the writing of his treatise *On Mortality*. It also appears to have been the reason for his writing an apologetic work to the pagan Demetrian since an event like a plague would tend to lead to suspicions of witchcraft by such groups as Christians and thus inspire a local persecution.[12] Under such a threat, a council that took place in Carthage in May 253 affirmed, notwithstanding the decisions of previous councils, that a general peace should be granted to all the penitent fallen, in view of the new persecution that threatened, in order to strengthen the faithful with the means of grace for the oncoming trial.[13]

Gallus appears to have confirmed expectations of renewing the persecution, at least in the case of Rome itself, where Cornelius was condemned to exile as a first stage in his trial of endurance.[14] Though Cyprian expected him to progress to a further examination and martyrdom in blood, his expectation was to remain unfulfilled. In June 253 he died of natural causes at Centumcellae on his way to face the magistrate, and was succeeded by Lucius.[15]

The controversial issue over baptism was to erupt when Lucius died after a short episcopate of eight months, and was, by early March 254, succeeded by Stephen. There ensued the famous dispute

---

[12]A. Brent, *The Imperial Cult and the Development of Church Order: Concepts and Images of Authority in Paganism and Early Christianity before the Age of Cyprian*, Supplements to Vigiliae Christianae 45 (Leiden: Brill, 1999), 104–105; 110–112. See also L. F. Janssen, "'Superstitio' and the Persecution of the Christians," *VC* 33.2 (1979): 131–59.

[13]Cyprian *Ep.*57.1.1–2.

[14]Sage, *Cyprian*, 284–86; G. Clarke, *The Letters of St Cyprian*, 4 vols., ACW 43, 44, 46 and 47 (New York: Newman Press, 1984, 1986, 1989), 3.4–17.

[15]Cyprian *Ep.* 60 and 61.

between the Pope of Africa and the Pope of Rome over the issue of whether someone baptised in schism or heresy needed to be re-baptised on the grounds of the invalidity of sacraments celebrated outside the Church. Cyprian's *Letters* 67–75 are taken up with this controversy, of which *Letters* 72, 73 and (by Firmilian) 75 are included in the companion volume to this edition, *On the Church: Select Letters,* by St Cyprian. In consequence, Stephen began to excommunicate Cyprian's Eastern allies.[16] The annual Carthaginian council of 256 was to support Cyprian's position against that of Stephen, as had the smaller council in the previous year.[17] We shall sketch in detail the basic issues of this controversy when we consider briefly Cyprian's doctrine of the Church (in §3 below).

In 253 Gallus was killed at Interama, in consequence of the Gothic campaign, by the rebel forces of Aemilianus. But by August or September 253 Valerian had ended this short reign. Valerian raised his son Gallienus, destined to succeed him, to the rank of Augustus. The following three years were years of disasters, and involved the difficult defense of both eastern and western frontiers.[18] But in August 257 they were to issue a joint edict that "those who do not follow the Roman religion ought to recognize Roman ceremonies."[19] The edict seemed to be directed against the clergy (presbyters and bishops) and church property, indeed against the very episcopal structure that Cyprian had strengthened and further defined.[20]

Thus Cyprian was summoned to appear before the governor (proconsul) of Africa, Aspasius Paternus, in Carthage on 30 August 257.[21] When demanded the names of the presbyters, Cyprian refused to give them. The proconsul then read the edict, which forbade Christians meeting or using their cemeteries. He then exiled

[16]Eusebius *Hist. eccl.* 7.5.4.

[17]Cyprian *Ep.* 70 and 74.

[18]Sage, *Cyprian,* 293–94, 337–41.

[19]H. Musurillo, *Acts of the Christian Martyrs. Introduction. Texts and Translations* (Oxford: Clarendon Press, 1972), 172 (=*Acta Procons.* 3.4).

[20]*Acta Procons.* 1.5.

[21]For a more detailed, secondary account see Sage, *Cyprian,* chap. 7.

Cyprian to Curubis. Significantly, pagan friends of both senatorial and of equestrian rank were to come to visit him, and to try to persuade him to go into hiding. Clearly he had maintained contacts with both the political and business leaders of Carthage, who no doubt had also been influential in securing the safety of his Decian exile. But this time the bishop of Carthage was not to flee. It would indeed have been difficult for him to argue on this occasion that he needed to flee in order to preserve the constancy of faith of the laity when initially it was only the clergy who were under direct attack.

In September 257 the exiled Cyprian had a vision in his sleep. A youth of more than human stature led Cyprian to the proconsul, who began immediately to write his verdict on a tablet that he be put to death. The youth indicated that in answer to Cyprian's request, a short stay of execution would be allowed. It was during this period that he wrote *Fortunatus on the subject of martyrdom, assembling consolatory proof texts from Scripture. In 258 Valerian strengthened his policy with a decree, with immediate punishment for clergy, and a policy of initial exile and confiscation for highborn Christians, with degradation from their rank followed finally by the Decian test.[22]

Thus Cyprian was recalled to Carthage in early September 258 for a new trial. Cyprian returned to his country estate (*horti*) when orders reached him that he was to be conducted by the military police (*commentarii*) to appear before the proconsul at Utica. He then went into hiding for a short time, so that he could make his confession in Carthage as bishop amongst the people in his own diocese. Thus only when the proconsul had arrived back in Carthage would Cyprian give himself up.[23]

On 14 September Galerius Maximus, now proconsul, heard his case in his palace or *praetorium*. Cyprian refused to perform the required sacrifice to the gods, and, as a Roman citizen, was sentenced to death by beheading.[24] He was now taken to the Ager

[22]Cyprian *Ep.* 80.1.2–3.
[23]Cyprian *Ep.* 81.1.1–4.
[24]*Acta Procons.* 4 and Pontius *Vita* 17.1–3. For the former, see Musurillo, *Acts*, 168–75.

Sexti, a large valley surrounded by a circle of trees.[25] Behaving like a Roman patrician to the last, he gave twenty-five gold coins (*aurei*) to his executioner. Behaving like a bishop, he handed his dalmatic to a presbyter and to a subdeacon. He tried to tie a blindfold to his eyes but could not, so a presbyter and a subdeacon came to his assistance. He placed his head upon the block, and the executioner wielded his sword with the required effect.[26]

Thus, to use the ancient title of a Metropolitan Bishop, Cyprian, Pope of Carthage, confounded his earlier critics and made his confession.

§2 Cyprian's Controversies

There were two principal controversies with which Cyprian was to deal. The first was over the conditions on which those who had lapsed or fallen[27] in the persecution could be re-admitted to the Eucharist. The second, which arose from principles that Cyprian had developed in connection with the first, was the question of whether there could be a valid sacrament of baptism in heretical and schismatic communities so that reconciliation with the Catholic Church would not require rebaptism. We will now consider a brief sketch of both controversies.

§2.1 *Absolution of the Fallen in Persecution*

In 249 the Emperor Philip had died in battle at Verona in Northern Italy and was succeeded by his opponent, Decius. The later adopted his own version of a typically third-century policy of proclaiming a new, returning golden age, in which ancient discipline would be

---

[25]*Acta Procons.* 5.2; Pontius *Vita* 18.2.
[26]*Acta Procons.* 5.5; Pontius *Vita* 18.3–4.
[27]*Lapsi* means "fallen" and I have translated it as such.

revived, and the unity of a disintegrating empire restored. Decius, as accordingly Trebonius and Valerian after him, was to continue the ideology of the *saeculum novum*.[28] We find on his coins, as of Trebonius Gallus and Volusian, the legend SAECVLVM NOVVM ("new age").[29] It was a tradition followed by Valerian, as evidenced by a coins from the mint of Rome with the inscription RESTITVTOR ORBIS ("restorer of the world"),[30] who also has a coin commemorating his *consecratio* (or "divination"), dedicated to *divo Valeriano* ("divine Valerian").[31]

Conformity was to be given religious impetus and sanction in the form of every Roman citizen sacrificing to the gods of the Roman state, principally the Capitoline Triad (Jupiter, Juno and Minerva), with whom the Decian coinage suggests that the dead and deified imperial families were conjoined. The peculiar character of a mint of coins celebrating the *divi*, or previous divinized emperors and their consorts, indicated the revival of the cult of collective worship of past emperors. Those emperors and empresses had been also associated with Jupiter and Juno on their coinage, in a religion in which the essences of individual divinities flowed into one another.[32]

Decius' edict to sacrifice was universal and worldwide. It was systematic in that it required clear evidence of sacrifice in the form of a *libellus* or certificate to say that one had conformed. Cyprian believed, and through his letter writing attempted to ensure, that the Christian response was worldwide. Christian bishops throughout the world were linked together in a web of intercommunion and mutual recognition. To be a member of the body of Christ you had to be in communion with a presbyter who was in communion with a bishop. To take part in the act of sacrifice, you sundered your union

---

[28]For Valerian as *restitutor* see H. Mattingly and E. A. Sydenham, *The Roman Imperial Coinage* (London: Spink, 1936), cited as *RIC* V.1: 42, n. 50; 47, nn. 116–119; 50, n. 149; 51, n. 171.

[29]*RIC* IV.3: 169, nn. 90–91, cf. n. 89; and 166, n. 71; 184, n. 222; 186, nn. 235–236.

[30]E.g. *RIC* V.1: 42, n. 50; 47, nn. 116–119; 51, n. 171.

[31]*RIC* V.1: 116, n. 7; 118, n. 24.

[32]Brent, *Imperial Cult*, 64–67.

with the body of Christ. The effect of these events on Cyprian's theology of the Church will be considered further below (in §3).

From his hiding place, Cyprian administered his Church through letters written to his presbyters and deacons, who were to remain at their posts. From such a vantage point he issued his instructions not to seek martyrdom, but if apprehended and challenged to refuse to sacrifice. This policy could not be as straightforwardly administered as he thought, with infringements punished by using the weapon of excommunication. There were degrees of conformity with many special cases, ranging from those who had sacrificed eagerly and without reservation; to those who had done so after imprisonment and torture; to those who had bribed a magistrate for a *libellus* (certificate) without actually sacrificing themselves; and finally, to those who were exempt because their husbands or fathers had sacrificed for the whole family in order to preserve them.[33]

The arrangement for ensuring the act of worship for obtaining the *pax deorum* was original and recent. According to Frend, it was the *Constitutio Antoniana* of the Severan Emperor that had made possible the order of a universal act of propitiation of the gods throughout the Roman Empire.[34] The existence of census and tax registers would make it possible to check names against official lists. Clarke is skeptical about the existence of such comprehensive documents. In the account of Dionysius of Alexandria, when the crowd gathered in conformity with the decrees and were called by name to sacrifice, was there in the magistrate's hand an official citizen list, or did they simply register their names themselves for the occasion, to be called out in order?[35] But however haphazard or thorough the means, the intention was to enforce a universal act that expressed the reassertion of the unity and order of all nations and peoples within

---

[33]Cyprian *Ep.* 55.17; *Laps.* 7–8, 13, 27–28.

[34]W. C. H. Frend, *Martyrdom and Persecution in the Early Church* (Oxford: Blackwell, 1965), 338.

[35]Clarke, *Letters of St Cyprian*, 1.33–34.

the one Empire. It was to be a sacrament of imperial unity that symbolized what it effected and effected what it symbolized.

The means for enforcing conformity were systematically worked out and systematically applied. Each citizen or even perhaps household slave[36] was to obtain a *libellus* or certificate of sacrifice, and we have 44 such *libelli* from Egypt, dated between 12 June and 14 July 250. From these we can gather that the local authorities had to appoint a given date for the sacrifices to the gods.[37] An examining board, consisting of local magistrates joined by five prominent local citizens would then be set up to place the orders into effect. First of all the subject mounted the hill to the temple of the Capitoline Triad and there he gave sacrificial meat to the pagan priest to be placed upon the altar, and poured a libation of wine. Instead he might prefer an offering of incense such as Pliny permitted to the emperor's image in order to give a minimal indication of submission to Rome's gods.[38] Secondly the petitioner now read out his declaration to the commissioners that he had sacrificed, and one or more of them signed the document as witnesses.[39]

In consequence we have two categories of apostates mentioned by Cyprian, namely the *sacrificati* ("those who had sacrificed") and *thurificati* ("those who had offered incense").[40] A third category consisted of those who never went up to the Capitoline Temple on the summit of the Byrsa, but bribed the magistrate instead to issue a certificate saying that they had. These were known as the *libellatici*.[41] For Cyprian all three groups had apostatised. Because the *sacrificati* had eaten idol meats, they could no longer be in communion with

---

[36]Cyprian *Ep. 15.4 implies that more than Roman citizens were involved since the martyr's *libellus pacis* (certificate of peace) named *liberti* (freedmen) and *domestici* (domestic slaves).

[37]J. R. Knipfing, "The Libelli of the Decian Persecution," *HTR* 16 (1923): 345–90.

[38]G. E. M. De Ste. Croix, "Why were the Early Christians Persecuted?—A Rejoinder," *Past and Present* 27 (1964): 28–33; cf. R. L. Wilken, *The Christians as the Romans Saw Them* (New Haven, CT and London: Yale University Press, 1984), 41–44.

[39]Clarke, *The Letters of St Cyprian*, 1.30–32.

[40]Cyprian *Ep.* 55.2.1, 12.1; *Laps.* 22–26.

[41]Cyprian *Ep.* 55.14.1–2; *Laps.* 27–30.

the Church that received the body and blood of Christ. Because the *thurificati* had offered incense to propitiate the gods, Christ's propitiation no longer availed. Though the *libellatici* had done neither of these things, nevertheless they had solemnly professed that they had done them before the commissioners signed their *libellus*. Accordingly they had fallen because they had denied their baptism, which involved their profession of the name of Christ. Behind such a view, as we shall later see (in §3), was Cyprian's corporate view of the Church. Baptism and Eucharist were the means for incorporation into the Church as the body of Christ. To receive pagan sacraments or to affirm falsely that one had received them was to sunder one's union in the body of Christ.

But Cyprian's position was further complicated by the existence of a group of confessors, or those who had confessed their faith unwaveringly and yet managed to survive without actually dying as martyrs. There were a large number of these in the Decian persecution, the aim of which was to secure apostates rather than martyrs in a process of savage re-education in ancient Roman discipline. These claimed the right to absolve the fallen and issued a *libellus pacis*, a certificate which declared them reconciled and at peace with the Church. Cyprian considered this a challenge to his authority, and his reasons against the practice he sets out in his treatise *On the Fallen* as well as in several of his *Letters*.[42] The practice of absolving by issuing a *libellus pacis* was indeed new, and clearly the counterpart to Decius' *libellus* of sacrifice. But the prerogatives of the martyrs to absolve by offering the Eucharistic sacrifice and communicating the penitent as the act of reconciliation per se, with the claim that they were ordained to the presbyterate by virtue of their confession without imposition of hands, may well have been of great antiquity.[43]

Whether separate from this group or as part of it, there arose a group of presbyters who themselves claimed the prerogative to

---

[42]*Ep.* 16 and 27, see also **Ep.* 17–20; 25–26.
[43]A. Brent, "Cyprian and the question of *ordinatio per confessionem*," StPatr 36 (2001): 323–37.

reconcile those who had fallen from their faith in persecution. Their action, like that of the martyrs with whom perhaps they were associated, was to cause controversy. Novatus in Africa and Novatian in Rome were to end up consecrated as rival bishops to Cyprian and Cornelius because they supported a rigorist position that would not re-admit anyone who had fallen to full communion, but insisted on a lifelong penitence. Cyprian took a mediating position between these groups, which he was in time to develop, and over which, to some extent, to vacillate. His position was that any decision on the reconciliation of the fallen must await a council to be summoned after the persecution was over. Meanwhile the fallen were to remain in a state of repentance, desirous of receiving the Eucharist but cut off from actually receiving it. If they wished to wash away the sin of apostasy, they could do so with their own blood whilst the persecution still raged.[44]

As his *Letters* progress, he changes his position. At first he is prepared only to re-admit a fallen person to communion on their deathbed and then only if they received a *libellus pacis* from a confessor.[45] Then he is prepared to admit a *libellaticus* after penance but only a *sacrificatus* on his deathbed. Finally, in 253, as I have already mentioned, Fortunatus and Felicissimus were deprived of any *raison d'être* by the decision of the Council of Carthage of that year to admit all penitent fallen, on the grounds that their period of penance had been long enough and that a new persecution required their strengthening with the grace of the sacraments in order to prevail.[46]

Novatian, at least, when writing in the name of the Roman presbyterate deprived of bishop Fabian following his martyrdom, initially supported Cyprian's position, without even mentioning the need for a confessor's *libellus*.[47] But in 251 the five presbyters who

[44]Cyprian *Ep. 19.2.3; cf. Ep. 55.4.1–3.
[45]Cyprian *Ep. 20.3.1–2.
[46]Cyprian *Ep. 57.1.2.
[47]Cyprian (Novatian) *Ep. 30.8; Sage, Cyprian, 250–52; Clarke, Letters of St Cyprian, 2.116–19; J. Patout Burns, Jr., Cyprian the Bishop (London-New York: Routledge, 2002), 34–41.

had opposed Cyprian, under the leadership of Privatus, bishop of Lambaesis and a deacon, Felicissimus, insisted that the fallen be re-admitted, and proceeded to excommunicate all those who remained in communion with Cyprian who at that time would refuse such reconciliation except on deathbeds. They were destined to set up a rival bishop when one of the five, Fortunatus, was consecrated bishop. Cyprian retorted in turn by excommunicating him and his group.[48]

Novatus had been the presbyter who appointed Fortunatus as his deacon.[49] It was subsequent to the council that finally met in 251, and its decisions on the fallen, that led to Novatian at Rome breaking with Cyprian on the grounds that the latter was too lax. Church politics were also involved, in that Cornelius had also been elected and consecrated bishop, and he had accepted the position of Cyprian's Carthaginian council. Novatus, the laxist Carthaginian presbyter, was now to join the newly consecrated, rigorist bishop Novatian in a marriage of convenience against Cyprian at Carthage and Cornelius at Rome.[50] Cornelius called a council at Rome in AD 253, perhaps contemporaneous with that at Carthage, and in both *fora* Novatian was condemned and excommunicated. The council decided that those who had bribed magistrates and not sacrificed (the *libellatici*) could be received back after examination of individual cases but not those who had actually sacrificed.[51] Cornelius gave the consent of his council. In consequence, the permanence of Novatian's schism was sealed, and his rival Church in his eyes legitimated. It was as a background to the controversies surrounding these councils that Cyprian composed *On the Fallen* and *The Unity of the Catholic Church*.

But following the council of 253, another dispute was to break out on the issue of the baptism or rebaptism of heretics and schismatics.

[48]Cyprian *Ep.* 41.2.1; see also *Ep.* 59.9.1.
[49]Cyprian *Ep.* 52.2.3.
[50]Sage, *Cyprian*, 229–30, 249–54.
[51]Cyprian *Ep.* 55.17.1–2; cf. 23.4. See also *Ep.* 28.1–3.

§2.2 *Baptism in Heresy or Schism*

The grounds on which Cyprian argues that schism is a denial of what the Eucharist effects are corporate and organic. It is not that schismatics fail to understand Eucharistic doctrine, but they are not part of the reality of what the Eucharist affirms about the corporate character of the Church:

> Our Lord's own sacrifices proclaim the truth of our com-
> mon agreement in Christ, bound together by the unshakable
> bond of filial love that cannot be broken. The Lord points
> to this truth that our people whom he bore are joined as
> one by calling the bread, kneaded and pressed together out
> of many grains, his very body. In like manner, he calls the
> wine, pressed out from so many clusters of individual grapes
> crushed together into one, his very own blood. Thus in the
> same way he points to the truth that we are one flock joined
> from being mixed together from a collection of individuals
> into a unity.[52]

Thus far Stephen will agree. There is nothing to suggest that his predecessor, Cornelius, was not in complete agreement with the Council of Carthage of May 252,[53] when it rebuffed Novatian's over-tures to reestablish communion between himself as bishop and the community over which he presided. The council would only allow him to return as an individual layperson and not as a bishop.[54] For Stephen, as for Cyprian, Novatian could not preside as High Priest and bishop at the Eucharist, nor would grace be obtained at his altar. But regarding the validity of baptism outside the Church Stephen and Cyprian were to profoundly disagree.

---

[52]Cyprian *Ep. 69.5.2; see also Ep. 63.13.1–2.
[53]For a discussion of this date and council, see Clarke, *Letters of St Cyprian*, 4.165–66, n. 9.
[54]Cyprian Ep. 72.2.1.

According to Cyprian, precisely because Novatian and his followers cannot validly celebrate the Eucharist, they cannot baptise. If therefore someone whom they have baptised wishes to be reconciled to a Catholic bishop, that is to say a bishop with whose network Cyprian is in communion, he must be baptised again. Indeed it is from Cyprian's point of view mistaken to speak of the "re-baptism" of heretics and schismatics since they were never truly baptised in the first place. Novatian's baptism is no true baptism but "a defiling deluge of pagan water."[55] Cyprian's views on baptism are expressed thus:

> The Lord declares and vindicates the principle in his gospel that only through those who possess the Holy Spirit can sins be absolved. But in baptism sins are absolved to everyone as an individual . . . Therefore, in this passage (Jn 20.21–23) he gives us the proof that only someone who possesses the Holy Spirit can grant baptism and the forgiveness of sins that accompanies it.[56]

How indeed was Stephen to reply to this carefully argued position, founded as it was on Cyprian's systematically worked out understanding of the Church as the body of Christ?[57]

Undoubtedly the tradition, as Stephen had received it, was that those baptised in heresy, and who were converted to Catholic Christianity, should be received through a rite of the imposition of hands by a bishop, with prayer, without repeating their baptism.[58] Cyprian's account of Stephen's position is:

> In addition to any arrogance that leads him to write inept and ill-judged claims that either are not relevant to the point

[55]Cyprian *Ep.* 72.1.1.
[56]Cyprian **Ep.* 69.11.1. See also *Ep.* 73.7.1 and **Ep.* 74.4.2.
[57]For an account of this controversy and the issues raised, see Sage, *Cyprian*, 299–335; Patout Burns, *Cyprian the Bishop*, 118–31.
[58]Eusebius *Hist. eccl.* 7.2.

that he is trying to make, or are mutually inconsistent with each other, he cannot resist this further statement: "If anyone therefore should approach you from some heresy or other, you should not introduce a novel practice but only what accords with tradition: you should lay hands on them in response to their expression of penitence. The heretics themselves, after all, do not administer their own idiosyncratic baptism to those who approach them, but simply admit them to communion."[59]

Stephen claimed that Cyprian was guilty of innovating in the light of his new theology and not giving heed to the tradition. As Eusebius says:

> But Stephen was angry with him, because he considered that one ought not to add anything more recent in contravention of the tradition that had strongly prevailed from the beginning.[60]

Cyprian however could claim African tradition on his side, against that of Rome. An earlier council had met somewhere in the shadows of the early-third century under Agrippinus, bishop of Carthage, and had held rebaptism of heretics to be necessary. The clear need for such a judgment showed that the denial of that necessity was widespread even in North Africa. In the council of 255, Cyprian's North African episcopal colleagues re-affirmed Cyprian's position.[61] But his *Letters,* written subsequent to that council, revealed widespread unease.[62] Another, larger council assembled in spring 256.[63]

[59]Cyprian *Ep.* 74.1.2.
[60]Eusebius *Hist. eccl.* 7.3.
[61]Cyprian *Ep.* 70.
[62]Cyprian *Ep.* 72–73. See also Sage, *Cyprian*, 309–11.
[63]Cyprian *Ep.* 72.1.1.

By autumn he had summoned a further council, whose Acts reveal an identical outcome.[64]

Stephen was to attempt a theological justification of that tradition, and of his own claims that tradition must be accepted. We can glimpse his case in what Cyprian says in his *Letters* 72–73, and Firmilian, bishop of Caesarea in Cappadocia, in *Letter* 75.[65] We also have the anonymous treatise *On the Rebaptism of Heretics*, which argues Stephen's case.[66] Basically, that case is as follows:

Heretics and schismatics, whilst not possessing the Holy Spirit, have been baptised into the Name of Jesus. As a result, they are renewed and sanctified.[67] If the name of Jesus is not invoked, then Stephen will agree that it is not Christian baptism, but this would neither be usually nor generally the case with schismatics and heretics. But they have not received with the name the Holy Spirit, which can only be imparted through the imposition of episcopal hands. Here Stephen appears to be commenting upon traditional baptismal practice, as witnessed by the Hippolytan school in the *Apostolic Tradition*. On Easter Eve, immediately before the baptismal rite is performed, the bishop lays hands on the catechumens. Then, in order to exorcise them, he breathes upon them (insufflation), and anoints them with the sign of the cross.[68] Were heretics re-admitted by the imposition of hands as a rite of exorcism? If so, Stephen claims the rite to be one, not of negative daemonic expulsion, but of positive insufflation of the Spirit.[69] We have here the genesis of the practice of the Western Church in separating baptism in infancy from the imposition of hands and anointing in a separate rite of confirmation

[64]Cyprian *Sententiae Episcoporum Numero LXXXVII De Haereticis Baptizandis,* in CCSL III E. (Turnhout: Brepols 2004).

[65]See also Cyprian *Ep.* 69–71 and 74.

[66]For the Latin text of that treatise, see G. Hartel, ed., *S. Thasci Caecili Cypriani, Opera Omnia*, Part III, V (Vienna 1871).

[67]Cyprian *Ep.* 74.5.1.

[68]Pseudo-Hippolytus *Trad. ap.* 20.8. See also Tertullian *Bapt.* 7–8. For these and other early texts, see E. C. Whitaker, *Documents of the Baptismal Liturgy* (London: SPCK 1960), 1–32.

[69]Cyprian *Ep.* 69.15.2.

at a later stage. Stephen certainly distinguished between giving the name of Christ and receiving the Spirit through the imposition of hands. Thus Cyprian will respond:

> Furthermore, no one is born by receiving the Holy Spirit through the imposition of hands, but through baptism. As in the case of the first man, Adam, only by being already born does he receive spirit: it was after God had moulded him that he breathed into him through his face the breath that gave him life. Some one must already be in living existence to be able to receive the Spirit; otherwise he cannot receive it. Birth, in the case of Christians, is at their baptism so that the act of giving birth in baptism and sanctification exists with the bride of Christ alone. She alone can conceive and give birth to sons for God. From whom else can someone who is a son of the Church have been born to God? Any one who has God as his Father must have had previously the Church as his Mother.[70]

Firmilian also supports Cyprian in his claim that Stephen held that heretical baptism can produce remission of sins and the Second Birth, even though he himself admits that heretics do not have the Holy Spirit.[71] Cyprian's final response, shared by Firmilian, is that Stephen is finally inconsistent: on the one hand Stephen will agree with his predecessors but one, Cornelius, that Novatian has founded an imitation Church with pseudo bishops who cannot therefore by their acts convey grace; on the other hand he will accept the validity of baptisms even though they have been performed in a sham Church. Firmilian thinks that he has found the *reductio ad absurdum* of Stephen's argument when he points to an example of baptism not simply performed by heretical men but by an heretical woman.

[70]Cyprian *Ep.* 74.7.1.
[71]Cyprian (Firmilian) *Ep.* 75.8.1.

Put in an anachronistic way that Cyprian's contemporaries might not have recognized, if the sacrament of baptism is valid amongst schismatics and heretics, then so is the sacrament of ordination to the ministry, or the sacrament of Holy Orders. Firmilian produces the example of a charismatic, woman presbyter who, at the end of the reign of Severus Alexander, under the proconsul Serenianus (AD 235), carried out baptisms.[72] His *reductio ad absurdum* would not convince everyone today: a schismatical Church is not held necessarily thereby to be a sham Church. Furthermore, in accepting the validity of baptism given in schism or heresy, the problem is raised as to why, therefore, the ordinations of those Churches cannot also be held to be valid.

Cyprian, it must be acknowledged, for all his stringency, held a more coherent theology of the Church and sacraments than did Stephen. It was the role of his successors to try to prove the consistency and quality of his arguments in defense of the tradition, in terms of which, despite their radical brilliance, Cyprian's were clearly theological innovations.

§3 Cyprian on the Church

Cyprian's understanding of the Church as the body of Christ is thus fundamentally Pauline. The Church is organic and collective, to which one's existence, as an individual, is subsidiary. There is one body and one Spirit, within which we have purpose and significance by being individual members who contribute to the life of the whole. One example of this is found when Cyprian writes (probably in AD 253) his letter to eight bishops who had sought financial assistance to pay ransom for Christian captives taken in barbarian raids. The grounds for Christian compassion are expressed in the following passage:

[72]Cyprian (Firmilian) *Ep.* 75.10.5.

For who would not grieve in calamities of this kind or who would not reckon his brother's grief as his very own? Paul himself is speaking when he says: "If one member suffers, the remaining members suffer together with him; and if one member rejoices, the remaining members rejoice together with him," and in another place, he says: "Who becomes weak, and I am not made weak?" Wherefore now we must reckon the captivity of our brothers to be our captivity, and the grief of those at risk we must account as our own grief, since in consequence of our union there is one Body, and not only love's yearning but also our religious obligation ought to spur us on and enable us to pay our brothers' ransom, who are members of ourselves.[73]

But Paul will speak of an individual believer as having an individual body which is a Temple, and which he must not defile with idolatry or fornication. The question of defilement is individual for Paul and not necessarily corporate. Thus in this letter also Cyprian will go on to speak of the captives as being, individually, "captive temples of God." But Cyprian generally speaks of the Church collectively also as a body that is in danger of contracting defilement. On such a view, the defilement of one member of the body can defile the whole body. For Cyprian, unlike for Paul, it is not simply a question of "if one member suffers all the members suffer," but also, we may say, "if one member is defiled then all the members are defiled." This principle was articulated clearly originally in connection with participation in pagan sacrifices. Those who had thus apostatized and eaten of the sacrifice are described thusly: "returning from the altars of the devil they approach the sacrament of the Lord with hands filthy and tainted with the roasting smell of the sacrifice . . . they are on the point of invading the body of the Lord."[74] It is the

---

[73]Cyprian *Ep.*, 62.1.1–2, quoting 1 Cor 12.26 and 2 Cor 11.29 respectively.
[74]Cyprian *Laps.* 15, quoting 1 Cor 10.20 and 1 Cor 11.27.

corporate Church as the body of Christ that they have thus contaminated and invaded.[75]

Such was the rigorist line taken also by Novatian and his followers that emphasized the permanent exclusion of those who would contaminate the body of Christ by their apostasy. Cyprian earlier supported such a rigorist line, which he considerably mitigated when he came to support Cornelius against Novatian.[76] But his theological assumption of the danger of corporate defilement from a defiled member nevertheless remains. The fallen are allowed absolution following confession after the persecution, and in consequence of Cyprian's promised episcopal council. They are to come in penitence and are likened to those receiving treatment from a doctor. As a result of his period of penitence, the diseased member receives healing so that he will no longer contaminate the ecclesial body corporate.[77]

Cyprian will however extend his concept of invading the corporate body from those who commit apostasy to schismatics such as Felicissimus or Novatian, whom he will not distinguish from heretics. It is not their teaching that corrupts, but their dividing the Church, which is Christ's seamless robe. Yet irresistibly here too Cyprian will introduced the concept of contamination of the corporate body through contamination by an individual member. Quoting Num 16.26, Cyprian concludes:

> The faithful are not to allow themselves to be seduced by the idea that they are immune to catching the disease from a bishop whilst having communion with him in his sin. They are acting in collusion with the exercise of an episcopal presidency that is illegal and contrary to justice.[78]

---

[75]Cyprian *Laps.* 10.
[76]Cyprian *Ep.* 55.4.2, quoting *Ep.* 19.2.3.
[77]Cyprian *Ep.*68.4.1.
[78]Cyprian *Ep.* 67.3.1.

It is for this reason that, in the case of a schismatical bishop: "every follower without exception is to be linked in their punishment with his leaders in that he has been defiled with their sin."[79]

Thus whether they are heretics or schismatics, the very damage that they do outside the Church is not principally the dissemination of false teaching, as if the episcopal succession was simply a succession of true teachers, as Irenaeus had suggested.[80] If so, it would not be difficult to lambaste Marcion and Valentinus, as Cyprian does. But it would be difficult to include Novatian and Felicissimus on such heretical grounds, since they had no doctrinal differences with Cyprian. Their inability to give salvation to their adherents was that they had no communion with the corporate body of Christ so that they could not transmit the grace that they pretended. In Jn 20.22–23 Christ breathed into the disciples the Holy Spirit and commissioned them to forgive sins. For Cyprian, what is corporately given can only be corporately transmitted, and through bishops in succession—with whom he identified the disciples in this passage. This is why, in his letter to Iubaianus, he must deny the validity of baptism by either schismatics or heretics.[81]

Novatian and his followers cannot claim to be organically united with the inbreathed body of Christ founded at the Johannine Pentecost. Because they are not, any act or affirmation, however orthodox it might appear, is a sham imitation devoid of power.[82] Thus we may say that from the Pauline image of the Church as the body of Christ, and the Johannine image of the Church as the community corporately inbreathed with the Holy Spirit by the risen Christ, Cyprian derives the theology of the Church that he expresses to Puppianus in such terms as:

[79]Cyprian *Ep. 69.9.1–2.
[80]Irenaeus Haer. 3.3.1–3.
[81]Cyprian Ep. 73.7.2.
[82]Cyprian Ep. 73.2.1.

The Peter who is speaking in this passage (Jn 6.68–70) is he upon whom the Church had been built. It is he who teaches in the name of the Church . . . that the Church herself does not depart from Christ. The Church is a people united with its sacred bishop and a flock that stands behind its own shepherd. The conclusion you should therefore draw is that the bishop is in the Church and the Church is in the bishop: if any one is not with the bishop he is not in the Church. It is vain for some to let themselves be seduced by the idea that they can lurk in corners and be in secret communion with certain persons without being reconciled with God's sacred bishops. The Catholic Church is one, and cannot be rent asunder nor divided. Rather it is everywhere interconnected and joined by the glue of sacred bishops mutually adhering together with one another.[83]

However, there is a problem with Cyprian's move to such a position on the basis of such Pauline and Johannine texts. Cyprian's theology may not be unfairly expressed as follows:

1. To be a Christian, you must be a member of the Church, and thus incorporated or made part of Christ's mystical body.
2. Without that incorporation, you cannot receive the Spirit.
3. In order to be so incorporated, you must be in communion with a priest who is in communion with a bishop.
4. In turn that bishop must be in communion with all other true bishops, whose mutual recognition is the glue that binds all in the "bond of charity."

However, according to many contemporary exegetes, points 3 and 4 do not necessarily follow from 1 and 2. Neither the Pauline nor

[83]Cyprian *Ep.* 66.8.3.

Johannine communities knew of a threefold hierarchy of bishop, presbyters (priests), and deacons, nor of a network of bishops mutually accepting each other's authority on the basis of councils from time to time laying down certain basic ground rules.

Many scholars would argue that Paul's early communities were charismatic communities.[84] A community as the body of Christ was created by the contagion of the Spirit in life and doctrine from one believer to another, whose many members were united by the same Spirit in a self-authenticating society, which did not need the validation of an external apostolic succession.[85] Similarly Schweizer argued that the Johannine community was originally a charismatic community, in consequence of the fact, amongst other things, that the Twelve in the Upper Room are always disciples and never described as apostles. Why cannot therefore the Church as the body of Christ be understood as such a self-authenticating movement of the Spirit, creating new communities without hierarchy, in which every Spirit filled believer receives the power to absolve?

Cyprian has not the fruits, if such they be, of modern literary criticism of the Fourth Gospel, which would see the Petrine passages, principally John 21, as the later imposition of a hierarchical principal in which Peter as a named individual receives the ministry of teaching and preserving the flock.[86] Thus he would introduce, understandably, his first reply to our criticism in the form of the figure of Peter, entrusted by divine commandment with the care of the Church. From the unifying figure of Peter, who stands as the one

---

[84]E. Schweizer, "Der johannneische Kirchenbegriff," TU 73 (1959): 363–81, with which cf. A. Brent, *Cultural Episcopacy, with Special Reference to Contemporary Ecumenism*, Studies in Christian Mission 6 (Leiden: E. J. Brill, 1992), 73–80.

[85]I have argued elsewhere that even Ignatius of Antioch did not validate his threefold hierarchy in terms of an external apostolic chain reaching through secular history to the time of the apostles, see A. Brent, "History and Eschatological Mysticism in Ignatius of Antioch," *ETL* 65.4 (1989): 309–29.

[86]R. Bultmann, *The Gospel of John: A Commentary*, trans. G. R. Beasley-Murray (Oxford: Blackwell, 1971), 711–17.

bishop in every diocese, he derives his hierarchical principle from Scripture. Characteristically, quoting Jn 20.21–23, he says:

> After the resurrection he also speaks to the apostles saying: "As the Father has sent me, even I send you." After he had said this, he breathed into them and said, "Receive the Holy Spirit. If you remit anyone's sins, they are remitted to him, and if you retain his sins, they will be retained."[87]

It is "from this that we know" all that he claims about the unity of the episcopal college as the "glue" of the "bond of charity." We might concede to Cyprian this hierarchical principal, and add that of the bishop as successor of the Apostle Peter and to each succeeding bishop from him as source.[88] But we can still ask why there can in fact not be a collection of teachers in a given place, with different congregations, each claiming a teaching succession from Peter, and each exhibiting what Tertullian called *consanguinitas,* or a family resemblance, in their doctrine that indicated that they all received the grace of the Spirit by their participation in the mystical body of Christ.[89] Indeed, as has been argued elsewhere, the Roman community before Pontian, and the revolution initiated by Victor and Callistus that anteceded him, was a fractionalised group of house churches, in a loose bond of intercommunion. Each presiding presbyter-bishop over each house church had received the Holy Spirit and was handing on the orthodox teaching: there was no claim before Callistus that only one figure had authority to do so within a defined geographical space.[90]

---

[87]Cyprian *Ep.* 69.11.1. See also *Unit. eccl.* 4; *Ep.* 73.7.2.

[88]Cyprian *Ep.* 33.1.1.

[89]Tertullian *Praescr.* 32; cf. Brent, *Cultural Episcopacy*, 153–60.

[90]P. Lampe, *From Paul to Valentinus: Christians at Rome in the First Two Centuries*, trans. M. Steinhauser (Minneapolis. MN: Fortress Press, 2003 [German, 1989]); A. Brent, *Hippolytus and the Roman Church in the Third Century: Communities in Tension before the Emergence of a Monarch-Bishop, Supplements to Vigiliae Christianae* 31 (Leiden: E. J. Brill, 1995), 453–457; see also A. Stewart Sykes, introduction to

There is, therefore, an unexplained spatial and geographical dimension to Cyprian's argument that cannot be derived from his New Testament texts. The real determinant of the shape of his argument is the cultural background of Roman Carthage and its principles of polity and governance. The reason, never to be found in Pauline or Johannine theology, but which, nevertheless, shapes his exegesis of Scripture is the location of episcopal jurisdiction within a spatially bounded *imperium*.[91] There can be only one episcopal chair within a given *prouincia*. There can be only one legal and constitutional space with the consequence that, if Cornelius occupies such a space, Novatian cannot:

> So if the Church is with Novatian, she could not have been with Cornelius. But if on the other hand she was with Cornelius (who succeeded Bishop Fabian as a result of a quite lawful ordination) . . . Novatian cannot be in the Church neither can he be numbered amongst its bishops. This is the person who he has trampled upon the tradition handed on by the gospels and by the apostles. He is not anyone's successor. He has produced himself by his own action.[92]

Thus the Church for Cyprian can neither be understood on the model of a self-authenticating, Spirit-filled community, nor can it be understood as lead by presidents of philosophical schools in succession to one another.[93] Cyprian the convert, having experienced the

---

Hippolytus: On the Apostolic Tradition, Popular Patristics Series No. 22 (Crestwood, NY: St Vladimir's Seminary Press, 2001).

[91]For an account of the secularization of concepts of ecclesial authority in Cyprian, see E. F. Osborn, "Cyprian's Imagery," in *Antichthon* 7 (1973): 65–79.

[92]Cyprian **Ep.* 69.3.2.

[93]The technical terms in Greek for teachers as successors are διαδοχή and διαδόχοι. Presidents of philosophical schools are called προεστώτες, a term which in Latin is *praepositi* and therefore preserved by Cyprian but with a radically different, juridical meaning; see A. Brent, "Diogenes Laertius and the Apostolic Succession," *JEH* 44.3 (1993): 367–89 and Brent, *Hippolytus,* 475–502.

enlightenment of the laver of regeneration, was in denial about the continuing influence of Roman political theory upon his thought.

Thus Cyprian sought what Fahey has shown to be a contrived exegesis of Old Testament passages, in which what is shadowy and ill-formed in the New Testament is somehow better fulfilled in the Old, in reversal to what was usually the case.[94] He argues that the Old Testament type of schism is to be found in 2 Kgs 17.20, where the ten tribes split from Judah and Benjamin and set up an altar separate from that of Jerusalem. Likewise 1 Kgs 11.31–32, 36 is cited, in which the separation of the twelve tribes is symbolized by the act of the prophet Ahijah in dividing his robe.[95] Thus he is able to castigate Novatian as not only lacking an episcopal chair, but as offering sacrilegious sacrifices:

> He could not be admitted into our communion by any one of us. Novatian had attempted the erection of an altar outside the true sanctuary, and the establishment of a counterfeit Chair (*cathedra adultera*), in opposition to Cornelius whose ordination as bishop in the Catholic Church followed God's judgment and his election by the clergy and people. He was thus trying to offer up sacrilegious sacrifices (*sacrilegia*) in opposition to the priestly office of the true bishop . . .[96]

But subsequent to the reforms of Deuteronomy, the location of sacred, high priestly and political authority was, in the Old Testament, centered on one altar located in one place, Jerusalem. Cyprian envisages the bishops as high priests presiding over many altars in different, geographically determined places. Thus it is the imperial

---

[94] A. Brent, "Cyprian's Exegesis and Roman Political Rhetoric," in *L'Esegesi dei Padri Latini dale origini a Gregorio Magno*, in SE Aug 68 (2000): 145–58; cf. M. A. Fahey, *Cyprian and the Bible: A Study in Third-Century Exegesis*, Beiträge zur Geschichte der Biblischen Hermeneutik 9 (Tübingen: Mohr-Siebeck, 1971), 46.

[95] Cyprian *Unit. eccl.* 7.

[96] Cyprian *Ep.* 68.2.1.

ideal that leaves its final impress upon his theology, to which his scriptural exegesis is subservient.

For Cyprian there can be no salvation outside the Church as he has theologically defined it. For him Novatian can be no valid bishop because, cut off from the network of bishops in mutual recognition and intercommunion, he has no organic link either with the forgiveness or with the grace given to the Church in Mt 16.18 and Jn 20.22–23. Novatian and his presbyters cannot celebrate a valid Eucharist because their altar is both "outside the sanctuary (*profanus*)" and their chair is "counterfeit (*cathedra adultera*)." As a bishop already occupies the chair, with presbyters, deacons, and laity in communion with him, there is no sacred space within which the Eucharistic sacrifice can be validly offered.

We must now examine how such a theology of the Church is reflected in the debate both about the primacy of the bishop of Rome, and the controversy with Stephen on the issue of the rebaptism of schismatics and heretics that we have previously discussed (§2.2).

§4 Cyprian and Papal Primacy

Clearly Cyprian's theology of the Church seems to render unnecessary a pope of Rome as the guarantor of the unity of the Church. Cyprian views church unity as arising from a consensus on doctrine and discipline among each of the geographically located bishops throughout the Roman world. Episcopal councils expressed that consensus in concrete when they met from time to time to resolve controversies and affirm new decisions of individual bishops. It was also expressed in the way in which the new occupant of a vacant see was received into the college of bishops by an exchange of letters with bishops who may not have participated in their consecration.

Certainly Cyprian was actively involved in letter writing in order to determine whether Cornelius was the lawful bishop of Rome, namely whether he was the prior and therefore valid occupant of the bishop's chair, whether in other words he had been elected by the clergy and people, and whether others already ordained bishops had laid hands on him in consecration, and so forth. Furthermore Peter's Chair is the chair of any bishop in any diocese and not exclusively at Rome.

However, Cyprian is conscious of the tradition of Tertullian and Irenaeus that made the See of Rome analogous to that of the emperor as *princep,* or first citizen and leader of the Senate.[97] He will therefore speak of Novatian and his followers as beginning with Rome and going out to form their pseudo Church on the basis of pseudo bishops.[98] The Christian bishop of Rome finally was seen analogously with the pagan emperor of Rome as a result of Cyprian's abiding formation in the constitutional principles and laws governing the unity of civil society in the Roman Empire, despite the apparent ability of his theology of episcopacy to dispense with such a concept. Decius had, after all, expressed the strong ideology of the emperor and his family, through the imperial cult, constituting the divine principle of light and order and creating imperial unity and a new age (see above §2.1). But Cyprian was, as we shall shortly see, to modify his view of Roman primacy in the light of his dispute with Pope Stephen over rebaptising heretics.

Yet Cyprian, far from giving special deference to Cornelius after deciding the disputed election and consecration in his favour, criticises him as his equal. He writes to him a very critical letter about the way in which he allowed himself to be intimidated by the followers of the laxist Felicissimus, who had forced Cornelius to accept their letters requesting they be allowed into communion.[99] Certainly Benson, Archbishop of Canterbury at the close of the nineteenth century, used his account of Cyprian as a veiled criticism of Roman Catholicism in favor of what he regarded as the true Catholic order

---

[97]Irenaeus *Haer.* 3.2.2 and Tertullian *Praescr.* 44.14.
[98]Cyprian *Ep.* 59.14.1.
[99]Cyprian *Ep.* 59.2.1.

of his Anglican Church, before Roman encroachments upon his and his fellow bishops' proper, geographical spheres.[100]

The problem is that an ambiguity arises in the text of *Unit. eccl.* 4–5 because we have two versions, from two different sets of manuscripts, regarding Cyprian's exegesis of Mt 16.18 and Jn 20.21 in those chapters. One version claims that individual bishops are successors of other apostles, who nevertheless have "equal power (*parem . . . potestatem*)," but the bishop of the Roman Church is the successor of Peter who has the ministry of holding the unity of the whole college together as the "source of unity (*originem unitatis*)." The other, as we shall see, implies that each bishop, in his individual diocese, occupies the Chair of Peter, with whom, including the bishop of Rome, they were endowed with an equal fellowship of honour and power (*pari consortio praediti et honoris et potestatis*).[101] We shall shortly discuss further whether the pro-Roman passage represents a later, papalist rewriting of Cyprian's original text, or whether it was the first of two, original versions from his own hand (see below §6.3).[102]

Benson interpreted the more papal of the two manuscript traditions as a later, papalist forgery. More recently, Bévenot has argued with considerable conviction that both passages come from Cyprian's hand, but that the lukewarm version was written subsequent to Cyprian's dispute with Stephen, who was to succeed Cornelius after Lucius.[103]

[100]E.W. Benson, *Cyprian: His Life, His Times, His Work* (London: Macmillan, 1897), 186–221; 432–36.

[101]Cyprian *Unit. eccl.* 4.

[102]Recently Adolph has attempted to resolve Cyprian's ambiguity in favor of the view that he acknowledged Cornelius' primacy despite his hard words, in a way that I find unconvincing; see A. Adolph, *Die Theologie der Einheit der Kirche bei Cyprian*, Europäische Hochschulstudien 33.460 (Frankfurt am Main: Peter Lang, 1993).

[103]M. Bévenot, *St Cyprian's De Unitate Chap. 4 in the Light of the MSS*, Analecta Gregoriana 11 (Rome, 1937); idem, " 'Primatus Petro datur': St Cyprian on the Papacy," *JTS* 5 (1954): 19–35.

§5 Issues of Text and Translation

§5.1 *The Latin Edition*

The Latin edition used for these translations is from *Sancti Cypriani Episcopi Opera* in the *Series Latina* 3, 3 A, B and C of *Corpus Christianorum* (Turnholt: Brepols) and are as follows:

1. *De lapsis* and *De catholicae ecclesiae unitate* (*On the Fallen* and *On Unity*), M. Bévenot, ed., Part 1 (1957).
2. *Ad Donatum* and *Ad Demetrianum* (*To Donatus* and *To Demetrian*), M. Simonetti, ed., Part 2 (1976).
3. *Epistulae* (*Letters*), G. F. Diercks, ed., Parts 3.1 and 2 (1994 and 1996).

§5.2 *English Translations*

I draw attention here to some previous English Translations, which will be particularly relevant for those without Latin who may wish to refer to individual works not translated in this selection:

1. M. Bévenot, *St Cyprian: The Lapsed; The Unity of the Catholic Church,* ACW 25 (Westminster, MD/London: Newman Press/Longmans Green, 1957).
2. G. Clarke, *The Letters of St Cyprian*, 4 Vols., ACW 43, 44, 46 and 47 (Washington, D.C.: Newman Press, 1984, 1986 and 1989).
3. R. J. Deferrari et al., eds., *Saint Cyprian: Treatises*, FC 36 (New York: Catholic University of America Press, 1958).
4. R. B. Donna, ed., *Saint Cyprian: Letters (1–81)*, FC 51 (Washington, D.C.: Catholic University of America Press, 1958).

5. R. E. Wallis, *The Writings of Cyprian, Bishop of Carthage*, ANF 5.

§5.3 *The Textual Tradition*

Two essential families of manuscripts are identified through their relations to an established two versions thesis of the *De catholicae ecclesiae unitate* (*On the Unity of the Catholic Church*), chapters 4–5.

Bévenot focused on a manuscript that contained only the *Primacy Text* (*PT*) without any trace of the *Textus Receptus* (*TR*) that, as the name suggests, has very many witnesses. Clearly this was an essential move against a thesis like that of Benson who claimed that the *PT* was a later reworking of the received text and thus never existed in any pure form. It had no separate existence.[104] Benson's fallacy lay partly in the textual critics quest for a stemma at the root of which would be an archetypal *ms* of which other *mss* had been copies and the transcribing errors of their scribes the source of later corruptions.

But such a model rests upon the false assumption that scribes will continue within a single tradition of manuscripts, and that two or more traditions will continue their degenerating corruption in isolation from one another. Yet what happens in reality is that later scribes might actually refer to another tradition of manuscripts less contaminated, and seek to make some corrections from their knowledge of such manuscripts. At that point two consequences emerge:

(i) it becomes impossible to construct neatly two stemmas and to show that the source of one is derivative from the other because one cannot be sure that the scribe is incorporating another tradition or whether he is a witness to some third tradition with its own stemma, and,

[104]Benson, *Cyprian*.

(ii) there might be two stemmas heavily obscured by the coalescing of traditions in this way that lead back to a first and second edition of a work.

Both points were ignored by the approach of Benson that presupposed that there was only one true archetypal text of which later readings had to be construed as corruptions, accidental or intentional.

To simplify Bévenot's complex textual analysis in a form that, I appreciate, does it scant justice, we have several families of manuscripts that relate to *PT* and *TR* respectively.[105] The ultimate independence of the texts found opposite each other set out in two columns (Cyprian, *Unit. eccl.*, 4–5) is indicated by the existence of *PT* approximately as it stands in a single *ms.*, H or Paris *lat.* 15282. We therefore have four groups:

1. H alone with no trace of the version *TR*.
2. Two *mss* that contain both texts in immediate succession, first *PT* and then *TR*, but without any attempt by the scribe to amalgamate them into a single text. These are M (Munich *lat.* 208) and Q (*Troyes* 581).
3. Two *mss* that have *PT* followed by *TR* but whose last two sentences of the former replace those that they parallel in the middle of the latter, namely T (Vatican *Reg. Lat.* 116) and U (Oxford, Bodleian *Laud Misc.* 105).[106]
4. Finally we have *PT* but with insertions of two passages from *TR* and a word or two more in h (Leyden, Univ. *Voss lat. oct.* 7) and a whole series of *mss* in the same tradition.

---

[105]M. Bévenot, *The Tradition of Manuscripts: A Study in the Transmission of Cyprian's Treatises* (Oxford: Clarendon Press 1961), 56–57. For a full bibliography, see n. 3 to the commentary on *Unit. eccl.*, 4–5, below.

[106]Benson, *Cyprian*, 207 confidently claimed that the *mss* listed in 2 and 3 (except T) were "all copied from one lost ms which we may call the Archetype."

For an interpolationist thesis such as Benson's to succeed, it must, after all, have been *TR* that originally stood alone with evidence of a planned alteration of that text.[107] The evidence to the contrary however is of two distinct texts combined into one *ms*, and it is on this that the generally agreed modern position relies, following Bévenot.

[107] Benson, *Cyprian*, 200–209.

THE STRUGGLE
WITH PAGANISM

§1 *To Donatus*

Preface

Cyprian wrote this treatise a short time after his baptism and conversion around AD 246. It appears to have been written in order to convert pagans, and describes vividly the corruption of the present age, and the exhilaration of Cyprian's conversion experience of turning away and escaping from this. Cyprian shared a common perspective with contemporary paganism in the view that both nature and society were breaking up in a chaos whose roots were ultimately metaphysical. We shall see this common perspective, with its roots in Stoic philosophy, in high relief, when we come to his treatise To Demetrian *(6). There are no quotations from Scripture in this treatise, a feature which it shares with his* *That Idols are not Gods, *and which is indicative of the early character of both works.*

Commentary Chapters 1–3

Though Cyprian shows no inclination to argue exegetically from Scripture, he claimed to have rejected the culture of the age (2). Nevertheless he begins with a piece of highly stylized and quite affectedly flowery Latin, setting the scene for the dialogue that is clearly literary (1). We should not conclude, however, that this work is a complete fiction, and that there was no actual Donatus with whom the core of this discussion took place. Indeed, his bishop was named Donatus, as was another person, a presbyter, mentioned in **Ep.* 14.4. However, Cyprian has clearly constructed a highly polished, literary production out of the original conversation.

Cyprian is evidently at pains to emphasize his rejection of his secular formation revealed in the intended simplicity of what he is now writing.

Thus he prepares us for his description of baptismal regeneration with its complete changing of mind and heart. He emphasizes how difficult it is for someone having been accustomed to worldly esteem to give up the pleasures of public life that he graphically describes (3).

In discussing also in chapter 3 his state of sinfulness, he speaks of an innate and an acquired corruption, which should be read alongside his expression in *Ep. 64.5.2 about the "ancient contagion of sin."[1] It was Augustine who was to develop such ideas into a fully developed doctrine of original sin inherited by nature from Adam (Augustine Ep. 166).

Text Chapters 1–3

1. Cyprian paints an idyllic picture of autumn vintage time.

You are doing well to chide me, my dearest Donatus, for I remember that I had made a promise, and this is the seasonable season for such an account to be directly settled. One's mind is granted relief from tension allowed now that the grapes are gathered in, and can share a festive and still repose at the end of the year's weary round. My location as well fits the occasion. I am where the charming appearance of the gardens joins in concert with the gentle breezes of an enticing autumn to sooth and caress the senses.

Here one conducts one's day pleasantly in debates. Eager private discussions educate the heart's moral sense by means of divine precepts. Let us seek out this abode, that no ignorant judge may impede our eloquence nor the uncontrollable noise of the household din may deafen us. Let the neighboring thickets grant us seclusion, as the vine shoots stray and fall in hanging clusters and creep over the training bars that carry them. Here the roof of leaves forms from the vines a walkway.

Let us bend our ears to this concern. While we can look at the trees and at the vines, we delight our eyes with the enjoyable outlook,

[1]See also Firmilian's response to Cyprian preserved as *Ep.* 75.17.2.

and, at the same time, what we hear instructs, and what we contemplate nourishes. Despite the fact that your sole obligation, your sole responsibility, is discussion, you have nevertheless put beneath you the sensuous allurements of what you see, with that voice, with that mind, with which you are completely a listener, and with this love, in which you have found delight.

2. *Cyprian's language will be plain and unlike secular boastfulness.*

The small insignificance of my slender natural ability yields such slight fruit both in quality and quantity of what I may lay upon your heart. I cannot as it were produce piles of rich grass in quantity. But, nevertheless, I would press on with what power I can succeed, for the subject matter of my words is to my liking.

Let the claim to rich eloquence of those who boast be made in the law courts, in the public assembly, before the tribunal and by eloquent self-advertisement. Since our conversation is of the Lord, the sheer soundness of our discussion rests not on the powers of our eloquence to produce arguments eliciting credence but on facts. Here arguments are not delicately but strongly put. Our arguments are not embellished to charm the public ear with a polished speech, but they proclaim divine forgiveness in their raw truth without guile.

Receive and welcome what has come from experience before it is taught. What we will say has not been gathered over a long course of time, but is derived from what the work of grace has more quickly caused to grow by a far shorter process.

3. *Cyprian's former dilemma: the enticements of public life.*

Take my own example. I was prostrate at one time in the shadows and in the night of moral blindness, and at one time tossed on the high sea of this vainglorious age, and wavering in my wandering footsteps. I was then restless in ignorance of my way of life, estranged from truth and light.

I used to reflect upon, with regards to my moral behavior then and with an anguish that knew no relief, about what divine forgiveness was offering as its promise for my salvation. If anyone would be reborn anew, and inspired into new life through the laver of the saving waters, he should lay aside what he had lived before. Though his link with his body should remain, he should experience change in his human nature for his spirit and mind. "In what manner," I used to say, "was such a conversion possible?" Suddenly and swiftly that persistent decay either innately fixed in the substance of our nature, or to which, by its long possession of us, we had become so accustomed, would be stripped away.[2]

These reflections of mine penetrate deeply and profoundly right down to the root of the matter. Does anyone teach frugality when he has grown accustomed to dining at banquets and bountiful feasts? And when does someone, when continually seen in rich clothes and looking spectacular in his gold and purple, resign himself to wearing common and simple dress?

Some one whose delight has been to bear the rods[3] of the magistrate's office cannot allow himself to be both deprived of public honors and without adornment. It is because he considers solitude to be a punishment that he has packed the spectator boxes with clients. He is used to being honored with a regularly attending retinue of an

---

[2]The "old age" or "persistent decay" to which Cyprian refers in the phrase "persistent decay . . . to which, by its long possession of us (*usurpatum diu senio uetustatis*)" refers to what he will call in *Demetr. 3* the "*old age of the world (senectus mundi)*." He reflects the Stoic eschatology that nature as well as society has declined from the golden age to that of iron, and that both the earth and human bodies reflect this feature of the general decline in what was "innately fixed in the substance of our nature (*genuinum situ materiae naturalis*)." For discussion of Stoic determinism and its implications for nature and society, see J. M. Rist, *Stoic Philosophy* (Cambridge: Cambridge University Press, 1969), 175–85 and A. A. Long, *Stoic Studies* (Cambridge: Cambridge University Press, 1996), 40–44.

[3]Here, "rods" translate *fasces*, which along with the axes (*secures*), were the symbols of office of the higher magistrates (consuls, proconsuls, praetors and so forth) and signified the powers of corporal and capital punishment.

obliging procession. He must always have these enticements that he finds inseparable from his self-image, so has he become accustomed to them. Intoxication allures, arrogance inflates, anger inflames him, greed disturbs him, flattery seduces him, and sensual desire preoccupies his thoughts.[4]

COMMENTARY CHAPTERS 4–9

Cyprian will firstly focus on the moral qualities produced in consequence of baptismal regeneration, such as the change of values from those of present, secular society, inner assurance of forgiveness that brings peace and spiritual empowerment (4). But Cyprian goes on to insist that the transformation of the inner life and personal redemption is not all that is given. There is also the supernatural power that is able to confront the demonic in the sick that is witnessed as those born again perform exorcisms and effect cures.

There is there the empirical evidence for the New Birth, however much physical change in terms of the resurrection of the body might for the moment be concealed (5). Cyprian will return to this theme when he confronts the pagan Demetrian in evidence that his gods are impotent, and are in fact daemons that Christian exorcists control (*Demetr.* 15). Thus Cyprian can now contrast the new life of the baptised and its power with the world of paganism that he had with Donatus left.

The world is full of natural disasters and external enemies and unrest (6). But a disordered external nature is reflected, from Cyprian's pre-Enlightenment, popularly Stoic perspective, within both the individual and within human society itself. He turns to the bestiality of the arena, and of parents and siblings witnessing the success and hurt of their loved ones as gladiators (7). He denounces the theatre, somewhat puritanically, for perpetuating the memory of past outrageous crimes, and of teaching the ethics of adultery. Gods such as Venus and Jupiter embody the degenerate values imitated by their pagan worshippers (8). He thus concludes with a general condemnation of the hypocrisy of the conflict between public and private morality (9).

[4]Cyprian uses the common political rhetoric employed to destroy the reputation of an opponent who rejects the values of his contemporary society.

Text Chapters 4–9

4. Regeneration in the waters of baptism.

The things I describe so far often applied to me.[5] I myself was held and ensnared by so many errors of my former life that I did not believe that I could be stripped of them. Thus I was giving my obedience to vices that stuck fast to me, with despair about them becoming any better. I cherished my own evil actions just as if they were so peculiarly my own and inborn in me.

But the light from above shed itself into my heart sacrificially cleansed and its defilement removed, with the stain of my former world wiped clean with the aid of the water of regeneration. The Second Birth from heaven also restored me to a new humanity, when I had drunk in the Spirit. It was then that forthwith, strangely, in measure, things that I doubted were confirmed, what was closed became open, what was in the shadows shone with light. I was granted the means to resolve what previously seemed difficult.

It was possible to practice what I had thought impossible, so that I could now recognize that what had been previously carnally born, and lived subject to sins, and had been of this world, had begun to be of God: the Holy Spirit was now giving life. What death of that kind takes from us in repayment for our offences or what life of that kind takes of our virtues you will certainly know and recall with me. You know this yourself, and I need not preach about it. Boasting in order to gain praise for oneself is repugnant. One cannot boast but only be thankful for that which cannot be attributed to human ability but is proclaimed as from God's grace. In consequence, faith begins when we start not sinning, when our previous sinning was the consequence human waywardness.

---

[5] Does this mean that he was a *rhetor* or a magistrate? See G. W. Clarke, "The Secular Profession of St Cyprian of Carthage," *Latomus* 24 (1965): 633–38.

"It is of God," I assert, "everything that we are able to do is of God." From him we live, by him we are empowered, by him we have been so endowed with strength that we can interpret the signs of future events. Only let fear be the custodian of innocence in order that God who has flowed with tranquility into our minds with the rolling stream of heavenly pardon may be kept in the guest chamber of a heart that entertains him with a offering that is his due. Do not let freedom from care once you have received it make you be neglectful, and the old enemy creep back anew.

5. Spiritual, baptismal grace manifested in prophecy and exorcism.

However, if you keep to the path of innocence, of justice, with the firmness of your footsteps unfaltering, if, consecrated to God with all your strength and with all your heart, you become merely that which you have begun to be, you will be granted freedom of action according to the measure in which spiritual grace increases. For there is neither measure nor limit in grasping God's favour, as is the custom in earthly benefactions.

When the Spirit bountifully flows forth, it is suppressed by no boundaries and is not bridled by enclosing barriers within an established track of turning posts. It flows forth continually, it bursts forth abundantly to the extent that our heart thirsts for it and is open to it. We drink in overflowing grace in the degree to which we apply there a faith that is big enough. From that source we are endowed with the ability to quench warm poisonous secretions in order to provide curing medicine for the sick, on the condition that we have chastity committed to without excess, a mind refreshed, and a voice that is pure. We can thus cleanse the defects of foolish souls by restoring their health, we can command those reacting with hostility to us to be at peace, to be quiet instead of violent, gentle instead of savage.

We can compel those unclean and erring spirits, who have plunged themselves into human beings that they have subdued, to admit who they are by raining down upon them our threats. We can, like we were driving them with harsh whips, cause them to withdraw. We can lay them down to die as they fight with us, and they wail, and howl as we gradually increase their punishment. We flay them with our kind of scourges, and we roast them as with fire.

There our work is carried on but it is not seen: the blow is concealed but the punishment visible. Thus the Spirit that we have received controls at its own pleasure what we have begun to be. Because we have not yet experienced change in our body and its members, physical change up until now appears concealed under the clouds of this carnal age. But how great here and now is the empowerment of our human spirit, how great at the present time is its force!

It is not simply that our human spirit can withdraw itself from destructive contacts with the world, so that anyone who has received atonement and purification sustains no damage from the attacking enemy. Rather, our human spirit is made greater and stronger in its powers so that it has dominion by an imperial right over every attack of a raging adversary.

6. The present age is in chaos, as international events make clear.

And so in order that the proofs of the divine ministry might become more luminously clear with the truth laid bare, I will grant you light for your learning. Having banished the gloom of the evils of the deceptive world, I will unveil its shadows.

Imagine for a short time that you are drawn away to the lofty summit of a steep mountain, that you are observing from there the appearance of the objects laid out below you, and that you are gazing in different directions, with eyes outstretched, on the storms of this raging world. You yourself are free from earthly contacts. Then even you yourself will mourn for our age, and, admonishing yourself, and more grateful to God, you will give thanks with far greater joy that you will have escaped.

Look with discernment at highways closed by robbers, oceans blockaded by pirates, wars everywhere distinguished by the chill carnage of armed encampments. The world is intoxicated with each other's blood; and murder, when individuals commit it, is a crime: it is called courage when it is a corporate act. The largeness of one's ability to be cruel is what protects against punishment for one's crimes. An argument for innocence secures no freedom from such punishment.

7. Within the cities, gladiatorial displays reflect moral degeneracy.

If you now turn your eyes and countenance towards the cities, you find a death procession packed with people that make you even sadder than if you walked alone. The gladiatorial game is laid on so that the bloodshed might entertain eyes that reflect a merciless blood lust. Bodies are filled with strong food for energy, and limbs bulge with the firm weight of muscle fat. Thus fattened up for punishment, they can have a more expensive death. A man is slain for human sport. The ability to kill is a skill, it is an exercise, it is an art: wickedness is not only advertised but taught by the advertisement.

What, I must say, is more inhuman, what is harsher? The ability to destroy a man is a discipline, and destruction is fame. What kind of action is it, I ask you, when they throw themselves before wild beasts, though no one has made them do so, when they are in the flower of their life, with fine figure sufficiently becoming in their expensive clothes? Whilst still alive, they are decked out as a voluntary corpse, though pathetically they even pride themselves in their ills.

They fight against the beasts, not because of a crime committed, but because of their madness. Fathers are gazing at their own sons, their brother is penned in the arena, and their sister is at hand. The more bountiful magnificence of the show increases the price of the spectacle. But, disgracefully, the mother even pays it in order that she may share in her own sorrows. They do not stop to think that they are murders of their relatives with their eyes when they take part in shows that are as sacrilegious as they are harsh.

8. The portrayal of divinities in the theatre as a cause of moral evil.

From there turn your countenance towards examples of corruption that demand no less your repentance.

Theatre scenes, for example, which should cause you distress and shame. It is frightening[6] how tragic plays relive ancient outrages in their verse. These bring again to our minds, by the action of the play that is made to portray an image of the truth, the old horror of family murders and acts of incest. As a result, they do not allow the practice of the crime once committed to ever become obsolete in practice even though the centuries pass. People of all ages in the audience are reminded that what has been committed can still be done. Wrongs committed are never allowed to perish through the aging of the years. The criminal act is never buried by the passage of time. Wickedness is never allowed to finds its grave and be forgotten.

Examples are made of what have now ceased to be current crimes. Then there is the pleasure in the teaching of vile practices in these mimic productions. Either you recollect what has been done at home, or you hear what conduct could be done there, in the exhilaration of what you see. You learn to commit adultery while you are looking at it. Because the social influence of evil seduces people to commit vices, the matron, who perhaps had gone to the play chaste, returns from the play unchaste.

---

[6]*Cothurnus est tragicus. Cothurnus* literally is the high boot worn by an actor in a tragedy as opposed to the *soccus* worn by the comic actor. But it is extended to refer to the tragic play itself, for example in Juvenal *Sat.* 15.28. Since that is what it means here, I have chosen to translate the accompanying adjective *tragicus* as "frightening" in order to avoid tautology.

Next, as a result, what moral collapse, what kindling of the flames of disgraceful acts, what nourishments of vices! The suggestive movements of the actor cause defilement. You are gazing at spectacles that are contrary to the covenant and law of one's birth, at lustful submission, in process of elaboration, to an unchaste, vile practice.

Males are emasculated. All dignity and strength of the male sex is made effeminate by the disgracing of a body thus weakened. An actor pleases his audience there, when he diminishes his masculinity by behaving in a feminine fashion. He swells with pride from the applause that results from the lewd act, and is judged to be artistic rather than obscene. He is viewed with such pleasure for all his sacrilege.

This kind of person can make every suggestive gesture. He stirs the senses, he caresses the passions, and he assaults the steadfast conscience of a good soul. With this degree of willing reception, an audience is taken unaware by the lewdness of his suggestive influences. Corruption thus creeps up unwarily on an audience. They portray unchaste Venus, Mars as an adulterer, Jupiter himself, as an emperor of vices rather than of a kingdom. Inflamed by his earthly passions along with his very own thunderbolts, at one time he becomes white with the feathers of a swan, at another time he flows down in a golden shower, at another time he springs forth to abduct pubescent boys on the birds that are his servants.

Ask now whether such a spectator can be whole or chaste. They copy their gods whom they worship. The sacred rites of those wretched ones even become their transgressions.

9. The hypocrisy of public morality that is contradicted in private.

O if you were even able, placed on such a lofty vantage point, to intrude with your eyes into private apartments, to open the shut doors of bedrooms and to lay open their innermost sanctuaries to the examination of your eyes. You could then look upon the conduct of the unchaste which a chaste countenance is not able to look upon. You would see what it is a reproach to see, you would see what in the frenzy of their vices they in wild madness deny that have committed, and then hasten to commit.

Men rush upon men in unhealthy lusts. Things are done that are not able to bring peace to those who do them. I tell you no lies but there is a kind of character that chooses to rebuke others. Though he is a vile person himself, he chooses to attack the reputation of other vile people. He believes that he can get off as an accomplice as if his complicity were not sufficient to condemn him. The same people, who are accusers in public, are themselves equally guilty in secret though they have the responsibility of sitting in judgment. They censure publicly what they practice privately. They find pleasure in admitting what incriminates them by its admission. Their effrontery suits their vices and their shamelessness fits the behavior of the shameless. Do not be amazed at the character of their words: whatever crime their voices are admitting is nothing compared to what their faces are saying.

COMMENTARY CHAPTERS 10–13

Cyprian now turns his attention to the Forum that stands at the centre of every Roman city as the focal point of the administration of justice and the promulgation of law. Cannot these still be free from the corruption witnessed in international and in social life?

Cyprian points to the way in which the bronze tablets proclaiming the Twelve Tables on which Roman Law was founded are mocked by events that have taken place in the Forum. Factions warring over the imperial succession within the empire prior to the accession of Decius Trajan (AD 249) had seen men in military togas fighting one another outside of the law within Carthage, as with the Gordians in AD 238.[7] Any notion that his patron can

[7] See n. 9 below.

protect the individual as a result of the solemn obligations involved in that relationship are crushed by the reality of what is going on. Judges are bribed in a pattern of widespread corruption (10). Cyprian can now describe some examples of how the ambitious social climber must degrade and impoverish himself, with some interesting observations on patron-client relationships (11).[8] He now describes the uncertainty of riches pursued with greed (12). Even emperors themselves are not safe (13), an assertion for which Cyprian was supported by the recent history to which he has alluded.

TEXT CHAPTERS 10–13

10. Law and Justice are not exempt from the process of moral decline.

The roads are now filled with ambushes. Many kinds of battles occur, widely scattered abroad over the whole world. Gladiatorial and theatrical scenes have been witnessed, either bloody or sexually depraved. You have witnessed lewd acts of sexual desire, either exposed publicly in brothels, or enclosed within household walls. After all this, perhaps you will think the Forum free from blame over things more audaciously committed in proportion to their degree of concealment. Surely the Forum is free from the sores of injustices, and not polluted by any contacts with evils?

Direct your attention there. You will find there the many crimes that you abhor, so rather turn your eyes away also from there.

Granted the laws may be inscribed on the Twelve Tables, and the statutes are published publicly on a bronze tablet. Offences are committed in the practice of the law itself, crimes are committed even in the place where the statutes are published. Innocence is not safe there in the place of its defense. The fury of those in conflict with one another rages, and amongst the togas, when peace has

---

[8]C. A. Bobertz, "Patronage Networks and the Study of Ancient Christianity," StPatr 24 (1991): 20–27; idem, *Cyprian of Carthage as Patron: A Social and Historical Study of the Role of Bishop in the Ancient Christian Community of North Africa* (Ann Arbor, MI: UMI, 1993).

been ruptured, the Forum resounds with the ringing rage of disputes.[9] The spear is there, and the sword and executioner is waiting, the gouging torturer's claw, the stretching, horse-like rack, and the destroying fire. There are more tortures than body parts all for one single body of a human being.

Who in all this grants legal aid? The patron? But he is in collusion and acts deceptively. The judge? But he passes sentence for money. He who takes his seat for the purpose of punishing crimes allows them. In order that the innocent defendant might be ruined, the judge makes himself the guilty party. The whole place is ablaze with offences committed, and, generally, the harmful poison has its effect in debased minds with their various categories of sin.

One judge fraudulently replaces a will, another draws up a false document for criminal fraud. On the one hand children are summonsed to court for their inheritances, on the other hand strangers are granted their property. An opponent makes his allegations, the false accuser goes on the offensive, and a witness attacks a reputation. Both cases lead into false charges paid for in sheer audacity through bribes, when all the while the guilty do not face ruin with the innocent.

There is no fear of the law, of the president of the court, no anxiety about the judge's office. When you can buy something you do not fear it. Amongst so many guilty to be innocent is now the crime. Whoever does not imitate the wicked offends them. The statutes have come to allow crimes, and what is generally done begins to become legal. What self-respect is there in the situation, what integrity can there be, when there are none to condemn the unprincipled? You only come across those who should have been condemned and are not.

[9]Capellianus, for example, on behalf of the emperor Maximus had intervened against the revolt of Gordon I. In the process Carthage, having supported Gordon, was subjected to a reign of terror. In consequence, in Cyprian's own lifetime, Gordon III, avenging his grandfather, disbanded a legion and thereby provoked a revolt against himself at Carthage. See Herodian *Hist.* 7.8.9.1–9.9.11. See also M. Sage, *Cyprian*, Patristics Monographs Series 1 (Philadelphia, PA: Philadelphia Patristic Foundation, 1975), 37–46.

11. *The general pattern of social life and its corrupting networks.*

But we may perhaps seem to be choosing the worst examples. Are we in our zeal to be argumentative, encouraging your eyes to run over only those things whose sad and repugnant appearance gives offence only to someone who looks and speaks from the vantage point of a morally superior conscience?

So now let me show you what the present age in ignorance thinks is good. There what you will witness you ought to shun. You will now see what you think to be honors, what you think to be the ornaments of magisterial office,[10] the extravagance in being rich, the power that lies in a military command, the purple that reflects the magistrates' splendor, the power that resides in the unrestricted freedom of being in government. Nevertheless the poison of wickedness that charms you is a concealed poison. Evil when it smiles may even appear joyful, but its deceptive appearance is in reality a hidden disease.

Take the example of some drug that is consumed, when the draft appears to be of a fluid medicated with deceptive cunning, with flavored sweetness lacing its lethal juices. Once you have drained the dose down your throat, you react violently to the deadly poison that you have drunk. Thus you see some one whom you think to be illustrious in his very senatorial robe[11] and resplendent in its purple. With what spoils from his moral corruption did he make the purchase, in order that he might be so resplendent? What were the arrogant demands to which he acceded, made by those who claimed them as of right? At the entrance of what proud house did he lay siege each morning as his morning call?[12] In how many processions did

---

[10]"Ornaments . . . office" I use to translate *fasces*, which were the rods carried by magistrates who had power to punish corporally; see also n. 3.

[11]*amictu clariore* where *clarus* means literally "famous," or "bright," but also describes someone of senatorial rank when used in the superlative.

[12]"As his morning call" I use to translate *salutator*, which means "one who makes a morning call to his patron as a client." Here clearly Cyprian describes the practice of the ambitious and rising man seeking a patron to assist his aims. The support of a client for his patron had to include, by custom, such a sycophantic display.

his feet previously walk in humiliation as he pressed into a row of the clients on parade before he could now here and afterwards head his own procession? Now clients greet and attend *him*, but they are under no real obligation to the man but to his power. It is not from his moral qualities that he earns the right to be honored but from the badges of his office.[13]

You can finally see to what worthless end these things come. The sycophant, the timeserver, has now retired. The hanger-on is now a deserter who has dishonored his patron's position left exposed by retirement from office.[14] Now his conscience is torn apart by the wounds to his ravaged house now that he realizes the full losses of his drained family estate. It was at the expense of that estate that he purchased the support of his crowd of clients. He used this to strive for a transient popular favor with fleeting and empty promises. His wishes to provide something that the people did not welcome lead him to throw everything foolishly away for no purpose. Because of those wishes his holding office as a magistrate made him the loser, just because he longed for a spectacle that satisfied his vanity.

12. *The uncertainty of riches, sought by greed and to no purpose.*

There are those whom you consider rich when they join woodland glade with woodland glade, and who extend widely their estates without end or limit. They exclude the poor with their boundary fence, while they have a very great mass of silver and of gold and of great quantities of wealth. These exist in piles heaped up or in buried storage places.

---

[13]"From the badges of his office" is literally *fascibus* (from *fasces*) or "axes," for which see n. 3.

[14]The allusion is difficult but I take it as a military metaphor applied to a person retired from public office and with considerable less power, having been abandoned by clients who are no true friends. A deserter (*desertor*) on the battlefield weakens the flank or position (*latus*).

Even these people, surrounded by their wealth, are tormented by the anxiety of a future of uncertain expectation. They fear in case a brigand cleans them out, or an assassin attacks, or jealousy that threatens any well-to-do person should trouble them with groundless legal disputes. Neither does food nor sleep grant them security. One of them sighs in anguish at a banquet, though he drinks from a jeweled cup. When a soft couch after a banquet hides his drooping body in its deep folds, he lies awake on the pillow. The unhappy man fails to understand that these things are to him just glittering punishments, that he is held fast and tied to his gold, and that he is possessed by, rather than possessing, riches. When he is able to lift the burden from himself and lighten the load, he continues to brood over how his anxiety repays him. I am appalled at this blindness of the mind, and the darkness at the depth of such frenzied lust.

He persists in cleaving obstinately to the massed fortune that is the source of his punishment. There is no charity from him for his clients, since there is no distribution to those who are poor. Such people say that it is their own money, which they guard in a state of agitation, in physical stress, just as if it were someone else's, locked up at home. In consequence, they give no share to friends, or to children, or to finally themselves. They have possessions only to prevent others being allowed possessions. They call these things their "goods" from which they have no use except for evil ends. It is quite ridiculous that they should apply a name to such ends indicating something quite different from what they are.

13. The uncertainty of imperial power.

Can you possibly think that they are safe, that their unshakeable power at least frees them from care, as they shine in the splendor of a royal court with their sacred headbands[15] and their abundant

[15]"Sacred headbands" = *infulae* which were the headdress or white and red band of wool on a priest's forehead as the sign of religious consecration. There was

might? After all, they have the protection of the armed guard that surrounds them!

They have greater reason to fear than all others. A person is forced himself to be afraid in the proportion in which he is feared. There is an exacting punishment no less to be paid by the more powerful for a position of such eminence, for all his being kept free from danger by a numerous retinue, hedged around with a band of escorts, and his flank, enclosed and protected. In so far as he does not allow his subjects to be free from fear, so he cannot be free from fear himself.

Those others whom his power first terrorizes afterwards come to cause him fear in turn. He smiles in order that he might exercise cruelty. He flatters that he may deceive. He builds up so that he can depress. According to a certain principle of interest for the doing of injury, the more generous that the amount in payment for fame and honor, the greater is the interest on the debt exacted in compensation.

COMMENTARY CHAPTERS 14–16

Cyprian can now conclude with his Christian remedy for the age of anxiety that was the Roman Empire from 235 until his own day. Redemption is for him escape from the present age to heaven whose peace is above earthly uncertainty.

TEXT CHAPTERS 14–16

14. Escape from this present age is the only path to security.

There is therefore for Man one sure means to peace and to calm, one genuine and steadfast place of security. To find it a man must extricate himself from the storms of this restless age, and find his

no separation of sacred and secular functions in pagan society, and magistrates were also appointed to priestly offices.

anchor in a safe harbor. He raises his eyes from the world to heaven and gains admission to the Lord's favor. Nearer now in his mind to God, he rejoices that what might seem exalted and great in human affairs to others is now, in his heart's perception of things, laid low. He who has outgrown this age can now strive for nothing, miss nothing, from this age.

How firmly grounded, how unshakable is God's protection, how heavenly his fortification with its everlasting possessions. Through the same we are released from the snares of the world that entwine us, we are purified of the filth of earth for the light of an eternal immortality. The character of the craftily hidden infection of the enemy that previously troubled us and attacked us will be uncovered. We are driven more to love what we shall be, because we are allowed to know and condemn what we were.

No resources of wealth are required for this object, whether of corrupt graft or earned success, as if Man's highest honor and power could be provided by the labors of human effort. It is the gift from God, given for naught and willingly. Just as the sun shines of its own accord, the day gives its light, the fountain waters, the shower brings its light rain, so the celestial Spirit outpours itself. After a soul, gazing at the heaven, recognizes its own author, he himself begins to be that which he believes himself to be, higher than the sun and more exalted than all of this-worldly power.

15. Spiritual blessings in God's safe temple exceed earthly riches.

You, however, whom Heaven's command has marked for its spiritual military service, keep to the imperishable, the sober discipline in religious virtues. May your prayer or reading be often. At one time you speak with God, at another God with you. It is he who instructs you with his orders, it is he who stations you. Let no one make poor him whom he has made rich.

There can be no want now when once celestial food has satisfied hearts to the full. Then paneled ceilings embellished with gold, and houses covered with overlay slabs of costly marble will seem not good enough to you. You will realize now that you are to be adorned and decorated better than this. You are instead to be God's dwelling place, occupied by the Lord in place of a temple, in which the Holy Spirit has commenced his habitation. Let us paint this house with the colors of innocence, let us enlighten it with the light of justice.

This house will never fall into ruin over the long course of old age, nor will the color or gold of the wall deteriorate and be marred. Whatever things have been dyed on are liable to peel off. Things that do not reflect the true nature of what they contain fail to provide a stable guarantee to those who possess them. Things that abide do so with an adornment that continues unfading, with their distinctiveness untarnished, with their splendor permanent. These cannot be obliterated or wiped out, they can only be transformed as the body restores itself to something better.

16. In conclusion.

Here for now, dear Donatus, is our brief conclusion. Our conversation about salvation is pleasing to someone like you who has given it your attention with a patience born of the quality of your goodness. Your mind is firmly fixed on God, you feel the protection of your faith. Even so, everything that pleases you is also in the same measure pleasing to God.

We ought however to restrain our conversation, since as close friends our conversation is likely to be frequent. It is now a holiday rest, and our time is for leisure. Let us spend it in rejoicing for whatever part of the day is left as the sun now sinks towards evening. We shall not allow even the hour for dining to be without its share of heavenly grace. May our temperate dinner party be filled with the sound of a psalm! As you have an attentive memory and a musical voice, approach this duty, as is your custom. You entertain your dearest friends the more if what we hear is spiritual. May the sacred, soothing quality of our gathering charm our ears!

§2 To Demetrian

Preface

Demetrian was a pagan who had charged Christians with being responsible for upsetting the peace of the gods (pax deorum) *that the rites of Roman religion generally, as well as the sacrifices ordered by Decius' Edict, were believed to secure. The year* AD 252, *following plague, drought, and pestilence as well as external and internal warfare provided a favorable context for making such a charge. Cyprian defends Christianity on the grounds both that it is the immorality of the pagans who had secured God's anger, and because, in any case, the world in its 'old age' was progressing to its final decline. Here he shared in with his pagan contemporaries the perspective of an inevitable historical decline from an age of gold to that of iron before renewal can take place and the first state return. However, for Cyprian history was not cyclic, but had its final goal in Christ's Second Coming.*

Commentary Chapters 1–2

Cyprian claims to be addressing those pagans whom Demetrian has influenced, whilst giving him himself up as a lost cause. His words contain nothing but contempt for his supposed addressee (1). However, he does justify his actions from Scripture, which may suggest that his audience is in fact Christian, and he is seeking to reassure and console them under such an attack to whose logic some might have been tempted to succumb. Indeed, those Christians who had rushed to sacrifice when Decius' decree was first proclaimed might themselves have been influenced by the feeling that they should participate in an act that was intended to foster imperial peace and security in an uncertain world.[1] He sets out the charge that the Christians were responsible for the various disorders of nature that expressed the anger of the gods (2). Thus we see that, although the danger of formal persecution waged through an edict generally imposed throughout the empire had passed, nevertheless local persecutions could still break out in consequence of the pagan view that Christians represented dark forces upsetting the peace of the gods in whose cult they did not participate.

TEXT CHAPTERS 1–2

1. The pointlessness of pagan dialogue.

Being a man of discretion, Demetrian, I considered only with contempt your barking accusations made against God who is one and true, when your mouth was filled with sacrilege, and when you shouted continuously words of blasphemous abuse. I thought it better to show my disdain for the ignorance of one who misses the point than to rouse the mindless anger of a madman.

It is of course my custom to do this only under the authority of the divine teaching, since it is written: "Do not be willing to say anything in the ears of one who is unwise, lest when he hears he will laugh at your intelligent words" (Prov 23.9), and again, "Do not reply to the unwise in his lack of wisdom lest you become like him" (Prov 26.4). Also we are ordered to keep what has been sanctified within the knowledge of our private circle,[2] and it is not to be trampled on by pigs nor to be exposed to dogs. The Lord makes and expresses this point thus: "Do not give what has been sanctified to dogs nor cast forth your pearls before pigs lest they trample them with their feet" (Mt 7.6). You often come to me with an eagerness for making a case against me rather than with the intention of learning anything.

---

[1] See Cyprian *Laps.* 8.
[2] "Private knowledge" = *conscientia*, usually translated "conscience," but with this sense in, e.g., Tacitus *Hist.* 1.25: "the few who were complicit in their private knowledge of the crime (*in conscientiam facinoris pauci asciti*)."

On such occasions you prefer, sounding off shouted insults, to press your own case repeatedly and indecently rather than to listen to ours tolerantly.

It seems silly to engage with you when it would be easier and less effort to quell the billowing waves of a stormy sea with cries of protest than to restrain your rage by means of arguments. It is definitely a pointless task, and not liable to success, to present light to a blind man, speech to a deaf one, wisdom to one who is irrational, when the irrational man cannot think, nor the blind allow in the light, nor the deaf hear.

2. The charge: third-century catastrophes and divine anger.

These were my frequent reflections and I kept silent about them. But I overcame my reluctance and allowed myself to reply, though I may be unable to teach the unteachable nor to restrain the godless with the observance of the sacred, nor to keep a madman in check with moderation. You say that that we are responsible, that many complain both because wars are breaking out more frequently, because plague and famine are having their violent effects, and because clear weather conditions of long duration are delaying rain and showers. In that case I cannot keep silent any longer without our silence starting to become evidence of a lack of confidence in our cause, and not simply of a proper restraint.

As long as we continue to pay no regard to refuting false accusations, we seem to be admitting the charge. I am replying, therefore, to you, Demetrian, as well as to the others whom you no doubt have stirred up and have made your many associates in the dissemination of your hatred by means of the slanderous accusations that have grown from you as their root and source. I believe, notwithstanding, that these people would listen to the explanation of our account. For he who is influenced towards evil by a deceiver's lie will be influenced far more towards goodness by the truth.

Commentary Chapters 3–4

Cyprian here as elsewhere combines Christian apocalyptic expectation of Christ's Second Coming with Stoic views, held also by his pagan contemporaries, regarding the "old age of the world (*senectus mundi*)." Decline is written into the order of the natural world as well as that of society. Even without divine revelation, Demetrian ought to know this jointly accepted view of the world and thus not speak as if he knew nothing. According to myth, history was cyclic, and a golden age would always decline into one of silver and bronze and then iron. Stoicism justified philosophically the myth in the following way. All things had emerged from the primeval light and fire, whose congealment lead to air, earth, and water, and then to animals, men, and all other existent things. The primal fire was a material spirit that permeated all things, endowing their operation with rational order, and setting the determined path of a destiny from which no one could escape. Poseidonius and his followers produced an eschatology on such a basis in which all things arose from the primeval fire but were destined to return to it again, and thereafter to be reborn to their original condition. It is this account of nature as ordered by divine law that Cyprian calls "the law of God" (3).

Although history according to Cyprian's Christian eschatology moves towards a final goal and is not cyclic, nevertheless he shared with his pagan contemporaries a belief in decline in which the order of nature was collapsing into disorder before its final end. It should be remembered that human society was considered part of the natural order and not an artificial arrangement distinct from it as in the West from the Enlightenment onwards, so that cosmic collapse and moral collapse become two sides of a common coin.

Text Chapters 3–4

3. Disasters due to natural decline and the world's old age.

You have claimed that, because we no longer worship your gods, we should be made responsible for all those events in consequence of which the world is now in turmoil and is disturbed.

On this particular point, though you are ignorant of what God knows, and unfamiliar with the truth, you ought to have grasped in the first place that the world has at this point of time grown old. It no longer consists of those vital powers of which it previously consisted, nor is it endowed with the superior force and vitality with which it was endowed in the past. Even if we hold our peace and do not put forward any evidences from the Holy Scriptures and God's formal pronouncements, the world even now is telling its own story and bearing witness by producing the evidence[3] for its decline in the form of its own universal defects.

In winter there is not as great an abundance of rain storms for nourishing seeds as before, in summer the temperature does not reach normal oven heat for preparing the crops for ripening,[4] nor in the mild season of spring do the crops flourish as they did once, nor are the autumn crops so abundant as before with trees bearing fruit. There are less marble slabs brought forth from mountains that have been mined out and are exhausted. Their mines, hollowed out, now supply less wealth in silver and in gold, and their impoverished veins of metals run short as each day proceeds. The farm laborer grows less in number in the fields, and ceases to be available. The sailor at sea, similarly, has vanished, like the soldier in the barracks, integrity in the Forum, justice in the court, concord between friends in alliance, skill in practicing the arts, and moral order in practicing ethics.

Do you think that the constitution of a given thing that is growing old can prove itself to be of the same prevailing strength as it was able previously to be when tenderly young and lively? Whatever is at the point when its last end is drawing near, and sinking into its final

---

[3]"Production of evidence" = *probatio*, meaning generally "criterion" or "test," but used of the formal stage in a judicial process in Quintilian *Decl.* 269: "I know that this is the due order for a judicial process (*scio hunc esse ordinem probationis*) that I should begin by showing that I have a monetary means (*ut primum ostendam me habuisse pecuniam*)."

[4]"Preparing the crops for ripening" = *frugibus . . . torrendis. Torreo* usually means to "burn," or "parch" but is extended to mean to "bake" or "roast" in an oven, and so by extension here to the nurturing of food in the soil.

stage of decay, is of necessity growing smaller. So the sun at its setting sheds forth its rays with less brilliant and fiery radiance, so the moon, with the horns of its crescent fading, tapers as it wanders from its course. The tree that had been in time before green and fertile, now, with withered boughs, is in process of being soon barren, misshapen by old age. The fountain that used previously to flow freely and abundantly in overflowing streams, now failing through old age, scarcely trickles with scant drops. This is the sentence passed upon the world, this is the law of God: all things that rise as the sun must also set. All that grows should decline with age. All that are strong should grow weak, and that are great should grow smaller, and when they have grown weak and are smaller, they should reach their final end.

4. Natural history witnesses the world's decline.

You lay the charge against Christians because each individual part of the world in its old age is becoming emaciated. What if now the elderly should blame the Christians because they have less strength in their old age, because hearing with their ears is not as effective as before. There is no strength in walking with their feet, no clear sight from their eyes. The strength of their physical powers is failing, the vital fluid from their internal organs, the proportion of their body parts. Even though at one time the long span of life of humans progressed beyond eight hundred and nine hundred years, only with difficulty now can life reach the number one hundred.

We are seeing white hair on boys, their individual hairs fall out before they have a chance to grow, and one's lifetime does not cease in old age but begins with old age. So, at its very dawn, birth at the present time hastens to its premature end, so whatever now comes to birth declines due to the old age of the world itself. Consequently, no one ought to be amazed that individual and particular elements in the world have begun to run out, when already the world itself as a whole is in eclipse and at its final end.

Commentary Chapters 5–11

Cyprian can now argue that the metaphysical collapse into the age of iron, explained in terms of popular Stoicism, has a parallel and supporting explanation in terms of God's judgment of pagan sin (5). Evidence that God planned the present calamities can be found in Scripture (6–7). But the evidence of natural reason also here supports the Christian case against the pagans (8–9). If you look to moral disorder within, there you will see the true explanation of natural disorder in the universe, as a list of examples will show (10–11).

Text Chapters 5–11

5. Natural disasters are the result of God's judgment.

That wars follow frequently one another in succession, that drought and famine add to our anxiety, that our health is weakened by the outbreak of diseases, that the human race is laid waste by the ravages of plague, even this you should know has been predicted in most recent times. Evils would be multiplied and hostile forces move against each other. Now that the Day of Judgment is drawing near more and more, the judgment of God in his wrath is fuelling the flames of catastrophes upon the human race.

For those events do not occur in the way that your false witness and ignorance of the truth expresses in your insults and complaints. They occur rather, not because we do not worship *your* gods, but because you do not worship God. He himself is Lord and Governor of the world, and all things are administered by his supervision and direction: nothing can occur except by his action or concurrence. Consequently, without doubt, when those events occur which reveal the anger of God in his wrath, they do not happen because of *we* who are the worshippers of God, but they are inflicted because of *your* sins and just deserts. You do not seek God at all nor fear him, nor do you recognize the true religion, having abandoned your empty superstitions[5] in order that God who is one may be worshipped as one by all and entreated as such.

6. The present status of nature is foretold in Scripture.

Hear finally God speaking, himself instructing by his divine voice and admonishing us: "The Lord your God shall you worship," he says, "and him only shall you serve" (Deut 6.13). Again, "Be unwilling to walk after foreign gods that you should serve them, and lest you worship them; and lest you incite me to anger in the works of your hands to scatter you" (Deut 5.7). The prophet, filled with the Holy Spirit, bears witness to the same point and proclaims God's anger with the words: "These things says the Lord the almighty: 'For that time that my house has been deserted you have frequented each one his own house, on that account the sky will abstain from moisture and the earth shall withdraw its acts of giving birth, and I will draw a sword over the earth and over the corn and over the wine and over the olive and over men and over cattle and over all the labors of their hands'" (Jer 25.6). Another prophet repeats the same point with the words: "'And I will cause rain on one city, and upon another I will not cause rain. One part will be flooded, and one part that I will not cause floods upon will be made dry. And two and three cities will gather together into one city in order to drink water and shall not be quenched. And you do not turn to me,' says the Lord" (Hag 1.9–11).

[5] *Superstitio* as a depraved form of religion was characteristically used against the Christians themselves; see Pliny *Ep.* 10.96.8 and L. F. Janssen, "'Superstitio' and the Persecution of the Christians," *VC* 33.2 (1979): 131–59; S. Benko, "Pagan Criticisms of Christianity," *Aufstieg und Niedergang der römischen Welt: Geschichte und Kultur Roms im Spiegel der neueren Forschung,* H. Temporini and W. Haase, eds. (Berlin and New York: De Gruyter, 1980), 2.23.2, 1055–1118; A. Brent, *The Imperial Cult and the Development of Church Order: Concepts and Images of Authority in Paganism and Early Christianity before the Age of Cyprian, Supplements to Vigiliae Christianae* 45 (Leiden: E. J. Brill, 1999), 110–12.

7. The present state of nature reflects pagan sins and disobedience.

Behold, the Lord takes offence, and is angry, and threatens, because you do not turn to him. You are amazed, or you complain in this your stubbornness and scorn, if rain falls from on high so rarely, if the earth is caked with the dry remains of dust, if the barren earth brings forth with difficulty meager and discolored plants, if a hail storm falls and impairs the vineyard, if a whirlwind uproots and cuts down an olive tree, if a fountain is dried up, an unhealthy odor should spoil the air, a sickening disease wear down a human being. But all these events are the consequences of your sins that cause them.

God is roused to further anger when events of this kind and number achieve no successful outcome. For that those events take place either for moral training for acts of willful disobedience, or to punish evil acts, God declares in the Holy Scriptures, saying as much: "In vain I struck your sons, they did not accept moral training" (Jer 2.30). And the prophet, zealously attached to God and under his dictation, replies to these charges with the words: "You scourged them and they did not express pain: you have whipped them but they were unwilling to receive moral instruction" (Jer 5.3). Behold punishments are inflicted by divine appointment, and there is no fear of God. Behold scourging and whippings continue, and there is no sense of alarm, no dread. What if that providential judgment had no part in human affairs? How much greater then would be outrageous conduct amongst human beings that was freed from the consequence of wicked deeds because exemption was granted them from punishment?

8. The universe is rational and you must submit to its rational order.

You complain that the plentiful fountains and healthy atmosphere and frequent showers and fertile earth now yield less in their submission to you. Thus the natural elements are not serving their purpose for those ends that are to your advantage and that you desire. For you are subject to the service of the God by means of whom all things serve your purpose. You are subject to the commands of him at whose direction the universe comes under your command.

You yourself require subjection from your slave, and, as one human being to another, you force him to obey and be submissive, even though both of you share the same destiny of having to be born, a common physical state[6] of having to die, a shared, similar physical substance, a shared principle of rationality in your souls.[7] Through equal justice and a common natural law you both come into the world and afterwards make your exit from the world. Notwithstanding, if you are not served by him at your whim, if he does not yield subserviently to your will, as the dictatorial and excessive enforcer of his status as a slave, you scourge him, you whip him, you afflict him frequently with hunger, with thirst, with nakedness, and with the sword and with prison, and you torture him. Yet do you not acknowledge God as Lord when you yourself exercise thus your lordship?

9. Anger with God is inconsistent with both Scripture and divine reason.

Deservedly, therefore, the scourges and lashes of God do not fail to be present in the disasters that are striking us down. When these fail to accomplish anything in turning individuals to God by the

---

[6]"Physical state" is one meaning of *condicio*. For others, see chapter 19 and notes 12 and 13.

[7]"Shared principle of rationality" = *communis ratio* as a part of the Stoic doctrine of natural law in which the rational universe was reflected in reason in human beings; see e.g., Cicero *Leg.* 1.13.35: "We have been endowed and equipped with the gifts of the gods . . . that there is one principle by which men may live together and this is the same for all, and possessed equally by all (*parem communemque rationem*); and finally that all men are bound together . . . by a partnership in justice . . . How can we separate Law and Justice from Nature?" For Cyprian's popular Stoicism, see *Donatus* 3, n. 2.

great terror inspired by these calamities, there remains still waiting the eternal prison, and the continual flames, and the everlasting punishment.

The cries of pleas in mitigation will not be heard there, because here has remained unheard the terrifying voice of God who, in his wrath, proclaims his words through the prophet: "Hear the word of the Lord, sons of Israel, since the judgment of the Lord is against the inhabitants of the land, because there is neither compassion nor truth nor knowledge of God in the land; blasphemy and falsehood and murders and theft and adultery are spread throughout the land, they mingle blood with blood. Therefore the land will grieve with all its inhabitants, with the beasts of the field, with the snakes of the earth, with the birds of the sky, and the fish of the sea will fail, since no one exercises justice, no one pleads a case" (Hos 4.1–4).

God says that he is vexed because there is no knowledge of God on earth, and God is neither acknowledged nor feared. God protests at and condemns the sins of behaving falsely, of carnal desires, of deceitful acts, of cruelty, of irreligion, of theft, and no one turns to integrity. Behold, there has taken place what were previously prophesied by God's words, and, because of overconfidence in the present order of things, no one takes his advice to be concerned for the future. People have opportunity to be evil, in the face of these adversities at which the soul, reduced and constrained by the limits of time, is scarcely able to draw breath. In the face of so great dangers, they have the opportunity to direct a judgment at someone else in preference to themselves. We are angry that God is angry, as if we could earn merit for any goodness by living badly, as if all those events that have befallen us up till now were not less and of less significance than our sins.

10. Natural disorder in the universe is matched by moral disorder within.

Let you who are attempting to judge others now be judge of your own case. Look into the deep recesses of your conscience. Or rather examine yourself carefully, since indeed you have no shame about doing wrong, and you sin as if there was more pleasure in those sins themselves. You thus appear exposed and naked to everyone.

For you are either swollen with pride, or you are overwhelmed by greed or raging in anger, or unrestrained in your gambling, or drunken with much wine, or jealous with spite, or impure through sexual desire, or violent with cruelty. Yet why do you wonder why the anger of God grows as its fruit punishment for the human race when daily, sin, the reason for the punishment, grows?

You claim that an enemy has arisen, just as if you had no enemy already, that peace was possible in the midst of uniformed, triumphing generals. You claim that an enemy has arisen against you, as if at home, within your society, the false accusations and insults of powerful citizens were not raining down wildly and torrentially, like spears in an armed assault, despite external armies and dangers from the barbarians having been put down. You complain of barren soil and of hunger, as if drought made for greater hunger than greed, as if poverty did not grow more flagrantly, with greater intensity, from the search to increase marketable output and pile up the profits.

You complain that the sky has shut out the storm showers when your granaries on earth are tight shut. You complain that less things grow as if what are grown you are providing for those in need. You charge us with responsibility for disease and disaster. But with the very disease and disaster comes the exposure of the crimes of individuals and their increase. Meanwhile compassion is not shown to the sick, and greed and robbery cast longing eyes over the deceased. The same people avoid the funeral rites of their dead relatives, not having the courage to fulfill their family duty, and in eager pursuit for personal gain, they are covetous towards any possessions of the

dead that they can grab. It is clear that the afflicted have been abandoned in their sickness, and, perhaps, for this end, that they may
not be able to escape death by finding a cure. For one who seeks to
obtain by force the property of some one dying wishes him to die
from his sickness.

11. A list of examples of moral degeneracy.

So great a dread of catastrophes cannot give moral training for
integrity. No one among a people dying as a result of frequent disasters reflects that even he himself is mortal. People everywhere run
to and fro, they rob each other, they possess each other's property.
They make no pretence at not being engaged in plunder—there is
no hesitation about it, as if it were legal, as if they ought do it—as if
he who does not steal feels it to be to his own damage and loss. Thus
each and everyone hurries to rob with violence.

Amongst thieves there is in one way or another a feeling of
shame for their crimes. They love remote passes and isolated,
deserted places, and so it is there that they commit their wrong, so
that the crime of the wrongdoers is concealed in the shadows and
by night. Greed openly shows her fury. Greed in her shamelessness,
observed in the light of the market place, parades wantonly her arms
that flaunt her carnal desire. In consequence come forgers, poison-
ers; in consequence assassins in the middle of the city are so eager to
offend because they can offend without punishment.

A crime is admitted by the guilty, and no innocent person is
found who would exact the penalty. For the plaintiff and his witness
there is no fear. Wrongdoers achieve immunity from punishment,
while the virtuous keep silent, those who share their knowledge are
afraid, and those who are to pass judgment grant their services for
corrupt gain. For this reason the truth on this subject is exposed
through the prophet by means of the divine spirit and inspiration,
and he sets out a definite and plain argument, that God is able to

prevent adversities, but that he will not provide help for making the actions of sinners worthy to gain merit. "Surely," he says, "the hand of God does not prevail to make them safe, or will his ear be heavy that he does not hear them? But your sins cause the separation between you and God, and, because of your offences, he turns his face from you so that he is not merciful" (Is 59.2–3). Accordingly let your sins and offences be the subject of reflection, let the wounds of your conscience be the subject of serious thought. Let each and every one cease from complaining about God and about us, if only because they should understand that their suffering is merited.

COMMENTARY CHAPTERS 12–16

Pagan persecution, contrary to reason both in nature and in law, is therefore based upon an unreasonable claim that Christians provoke the gods to anger. The sacrifices of animals to gods that are in the likeness of baboons and crocodiles are not true worship at all (12). Furthermore, the persecutions were not justified in civil law any more than they were in natural law. Cyprian now turns to a defense that he has read in Tertullian, whom, according to Jerome (in *Vir. ill.* 53), he described as his "master or teacher (*magister*)."

Tertullian is commenting on Trajan's Letter to Pliny that appears first to have codified in law the fact that to be a Christian in itself was a crime, and not simply because if you were a Christian you were also guilty of associated crimes such as incest or cannibalism. After Pliny the prosecution no longer had to prove that such crimes had been committed, but simply that the accused bore the name of Christ. You do not need physical torture to win an argument if its logic is so overwhelming (13). If pagan gods have real power, then there is no need of persecution through a legal process: they will wreak their own vengeance on the guilty and not the innocent (14).

Those gods themselves have been shown to be daemons through the ministry of Christian exorcists (15). But without such a ministry, their own reason should have revealed to the pagans what Christian Scripture teaches, namely the irrationality as well as the irrelevance of worshipping idols that they have made of animals that face downwards, when God has created man upright (16).

TEXT CHAPTERS 12–16

12. Pagans persecute those who are innocent of causing divine anger.

Is not here the basic substance on which our account chiefly focuses, namely that you are harassing the innocent with your accusations, that you are fighting in a rough game against God, and that you are attempting to crush the servants of God? Is it of little point that your living is stained from different forms of wild vices, from the defilement of bestial crimes, from gain from robbery with bloody violence, that true religion has been overturned by false superstitions, that God is totally unsought and without fear? Up till now you harass, in unjust persecutions, the servants of God, who are dedicated to the grandeur of God and to his divine presence. It is not enough that you do not worship God yourself: in addition you pursue those who do worship him by sacrilegiously assaulting them.

You neither worship God nor allow him to be worshipped at all. The worshipper of God alone displeases you, when everyone else pleases you: you are delighted when they not only venerate silly images and statues made by human hand but also certain strange creatures and monsters. The ashes of dead sacrifices and the funeral pyres of animals[8] smoke everywhere in your temples, and the altars of a true God are either not in evidence or are hidden. Crocodiles, and dog-faced baboons, and stones and snakes, are worshipped. So the only true God on earth either is not worshipped, or that, when he is worshipped, punishments follow for his worshippers.

You deprive of their home those who are innocent, righteous, dear to God, you rob them of the wealth of their inheritance, you weigh them down with chains, you shut them in prison, you punish them with wild beasts, with the sword, with trial by fire. Nor is it

---

[8]"Ashes of dead sacrifices" = *hostiarum busta*, and "funeral pyres of animals" = *rogi pecorum. Bustum* and *rogus,* associated with remains in cremation and funerals, are here associated with pagan sacrifices in order to bring out their ineffectiveness or otherwise their death-bringing character for those who offer them.

enough for you to fast track our sufferings, with quick punishments of a simple and short duration. You protract the tortures that you apply over time to bodies that you are going to mutilate, you multiply numerous kinds of executions by cutting internal physical organs to pieces. Your savagery and your barbarity are unable to find satisfaction with customary instruments of torture: your natural gift of cruelty devises new punishments.

13. *The label "Christian" cannot prove guilt of itself apart from a crime.*

What is this insatiable frenzy for execution, what this overwhelming drive for a cruelty that cannot find satisfaction? Make then your preferred choice from these two: is it, or is it not a crime to be a Christian? If it is a crime, why do you not simply kill him who confesses it. If it is not a crime, why to you prosecute the innocent? For if I deny the charge, I have to be tortured. If, because I fear punishment, I should conceal, with a lie that deceives you, that which I was before, and that I do not worship your gods, then in that case I ought to be tortured. I ought then be forced into confession of the charge by the power of the pain, just as in other criminal investigations defendants who deny that they should be convicted for the charge of which they are accused are tortured.

It is usually only when that truth could not be obtained from a free and verbal admission that the truth of the charge is forced out of them by applying suffering to their body. But now to the contrary, when I confess willingly, and I proclaim and testify with the same repeated and continuous words "I am a Christian," why do you inflict tortures on me as I confess? I am using arguments that destroy your gods, not from certain secret hiding places but openly, but publicly, but in the Forum itself, in the hearing of magistrates and presiding judges. It is as if your criminal evidence stated previously against me had been worth so little that, out of hatred as well as punishment, you felt the obligation to make it grow more.

While I proclaim in a populous locality that I am a Christian, and with a crowd standing around, and I dismay both you and your gods in a plain, formal public proclamation, why should you direct yourself to making my body weak, why should you exert yourself against the fragility of earthly flesh? Exert your mind with greater vigor, show the invalidity and emptiness of the strong points of the intellectual case, undermine confidence in it, win the argument, if you can, by debating it, and win by rational argument.

14. If the gods have true divine power, then they can avenge themselves.

Indeed, if your gods possess a divine nature and power, let them arise to take their own vengeance, let them defend themselves by their own grandeur. How can they be superior to their worshippers if they are unable to defend their claims against those who do not worship them? For only if the rescued is stronger than his rescuer, you are greater than your gods.

If, however, you are greater than those whom you worship, you ought not to worship them, but to be worshipped by them. Thus it is *your* vengeance that protects *them* when it is *they* who have been harmed, in the way in which legal guardianship[9] is needed to protect the retarded[10] from perishing. You should be ashamed to worship those whom you yourself protect, you should be ashamed to hope for a guardian's protection from those whose safety is in your own hands.

[9]"Legal guardianship" = *tutela*, generally meaning "custody," or "guardianship," particularly in respect to minors or other person not legally competent to manage their own affairs. It is also applied to the tutelary deity of a city or ship that symbolically represents a community or crew, see *CIL* 13.939: ". . . he who has restored the temple of the tutelary goddess (QVI TEMPLUM DEAE TUTELAE REST[ituit])." Clearly Cyprian is arguing that the roles are the reversal of what logic requires if the worshippers have the function of protector over the objects of their worship.

[10]"Retarded" = *clausos*, which comes from *claudeo*, meaning "to limp," or "to be imperfect or wanting," and not from *cludeo* meaning "to close or shut up."

15. Evidence from exorcism of the daemonic character of pagan divinity.

If you were willing only to hear those gods and to see them, when they are commanded to depart by our exorcists. They are tortured by beatings of a spiritual character, and are catapulted from the bodies that they have possessed by means of our words. Howling and groaning with a human voice, and feeling the whips and lashes that result from the divine power, they make confession of their judgment that will come.

Come and acknowledge that what we say is true. Otherwise, continue having faith in those gods that you say that you worship! But if you thus wish to trust in yourself, you will be deceived. Whilst you listen to yourself while you are speaking these words, this daemon that has taken possession of your heart is speaking with your voice. It is he who has now darkened your mind with Ignorance's night. You will see making petitions to us those to whom you make petitions. It is we whom those whom you adore really fear. You will see them subject to our hands, overcome and trembling as captives, whom you regard and venerate as your masters. Certainly and truly you will be able to feel confusion in those errors of yours when you look around anxiously and hear that your gods on our interrogation immediately blurt out what is their character, and, even in your presence, they will be unable to conceal their tricks and deceits.

16. Man is created upright and should not bow towards the ground.

What weak mindedness is this not to stand in awe of the true God, or better, what blind and stupid insanity of those who have lost their reason! Not to come from darkness into light? For those caught in the snares of eternal death, to be unwilling to accept the hope of immortality! God's warning words are: "He who sacrifices to the gods will be rooted up, unless to God alone" (Ex 22.20) and again,

"They shall adore those whom their fingers have made, and a human being bows down and a man has abased himself, and I will not lift them up" (Is 2.8–9). Why do you bow and bend yourself to false gods, why do you make your enslaved body bend down before stupid statues and images of earth?

God made you to stand upright. All other living things are abased, the structure of their bodies turned downward towards the earth. But you stand drawn to your full height, and your countenance is raised towards the sky and its Master. Gaze thither, lift up your eyes thither, and seek for God in the heights. As you are able to be free from the lower regions, lift up your anxious heart to high and heavenly things. Why do you collapse on the ground in the Fall that brings death with the serpent whom you worship? Why do you slide into the ruin of the Devil at his instigation and in his company? Preserve the high position in which you were born!

Persevere as the kind of person that you have been made by God. Stand your spirit upright in consistency with the position of your lips and body. Since you are able to come to know God, come to know yourself beforehand! God, if you plead with him, comes to your aid. Believe in Christ, whom the Father sent to make us alive and to restore us! Cease from injuring the servants of God and of Christ by your persecutions, whom the vengeance of God will defend when they are injured!

Commentary Chapters 17–20

Cyprian now argues that the Christian's submissiveness to persecution without resistance is born of the confidence that God's vindication of them is certain. Christians therefore view the character of the disasters differently. Recent natural and civic disasters are in fact evidence, not of God's anger against the Christians, but of God's vindication of them against the pagans (17). Because of the Christian desire for the spiritual rewards of the world to come, pain and death are not punishments, but means to realizing the purpose of life (18). Demetrian has therefore grossly misinterpreted the fact that

Christians share in and experience the sufferings from the disasters, social and natural, in the same way as the pagans. Though they remain physically and socially in a common body with the rest of mankind, they are destined to separate from that body at the end of the age (19). Their present sufferings are foretold in Scripture so that they can look with joyful confidence to their future state (20).

TEXT CHAPTERS 17–20

17. Christian certainty of vindication produces a pacific character.

This then is the reason why all of our people, when arrested, do not offer resistance, nor, though extraordinarily great and large in numbers, do they take revenge against your unjust violence. We can afford to be tolerant in the light of our assurance about the vengeance that is to follow in consequence. The innocent yield to the guilty, the guiltless accept quietly punishment and forms of torture, convinced and confident that whatever we suffer will not remain unavenged.

By as much as the injury from persecution was great, by so much the greater and more significant will be the exaction of retribution for the persecution. The wickedness of the godless will never make an assault upon our name that will not be divinely accompanied by an imminent exaction of retribution. We won't make reference to old records, and bring up again acts of retribution often repeated. We won't crow publicly about them in defense of God's worshippers. Rather, the evidence of a recent action is sufficient proof.[11]

God's action in our defense has recently and crushingly followed swiftly and with great speed: it can be seen in the natural catastrophes, in the diminution of resources, in the loss of soldiers, in the

---

[11]Though he might have been more specific, Cyprian is here referring to the plague that was the subject of Demetrian's attack upon the Christians. Cyprian is here rejoining that the plague, like other natural disasters, was the fault of the pagans and their sacrilegious behavior.

decrease in the armed forces. Nor should anyone consider that this took place by accident or think that it happened by chance, since, already previously, divine Scripture had stated and said: "'Vengeance is mine, I will repay,' says the Lord'" (Rom 12.19; Deut 32.35), and the Holy Spirit forewarns with the words: "You shall not say: 'I will avenge me of my enemy,' but wait upon the Lord that he might be your help" (Prov 20.22). In consequence it is clear and public that all those events that come down from God's anger do not happen because of us but to defend us.

18. Disasters are for Christians different kinds of events than for pagans.

No one should be thinking that the events that have occurred refute the Christian position because of the fact that the Christians themselves are affected adversely by the events that overwhelm them. The man whose every joy and fame is in this world is the one who feels pain from this world's adversities. That sort mourns and sheds his tears if he should experience evil in this age. For him there can be no benefit after this age, the enjoyments of living that comprise his entire experience. His comfort is confined entirely within this world, his fleeting and brief life here having an eye to some or other pleasure or carnal desire. Only punishment is left to give him pain when he leaves this life.

On the other hand, there is no pain from the outbreak of present evils for those who have confidence in future good things. In sum, we are not terrified by adverse events, nor are we crushed by them, nor do we grieve about them, nor do we complain in any natural disaster or physical sickness. Living by the Spirit rather than the flesh, we overcome weakness of the body with strength of the soul. We know and are confident that we are being tested and strengthened by means of those very disasters that place you on the rack and harass you.

19. Adversities do not affect Christians like pagans.

Do you think that we suffer adversities in the same manner as you do even though you must see that the same adversities do not bear the same weight in our case as in yours? Your lack of endurance expresses itself always in shouts of complaint, but our endurance, exercised in an unassuming fashion, is always brave and reverent, and expressed with gratitude towards God. Our endurance does not claim for itself anything from here that brings it joy or prosperity. But with gentleness and mildness, constant against all the whirling currents of this storm tossed world, our endurance awaits the time of divine promise.

For as long as our body continues here with a nature shared with the rest of mankind, it is necessary that there should be a covenant[12] to keep us together in a common body under which it is not allowed that members of humanity should split from one another into two opposing parts without first departing hither from this age. For this period we are confined together, both good and bad, within one house. We put up with whatever will happen within that house due to a fortune that we share, until that time of this present age has been fulfilled. Then we shall be separated one from another for the dwellings of either eternal death or those of immortality.

We are not therefore your peers and equals simply because, placed up till now in the same world and in this same flesh, we encounter with you equally the misfortunes of the world and of the flesh. For since every punishment contains a feeling of pain, it is clear that a person who does not feel your pain does not share your punishment.

---

[12]"Covenant" is another meaning of *condicio*; see also chaps. 8 and 21, and nn. 6 and 13.

20. Christians look for a heavenly paradise beyond earthly famine.

Hope's strength and faith's sure foundation is in full flower with us. Our mind is lifted up, and our courage unshaken, amongst those disasters of an age in decline. Our endurance is always exercised with expressions of joy, and, regarding God, our soul is always free from anxiety, even as the Holy Spirit says and exhorts through the prophet, strengthening the sure foundation of our hope and faith with his heavenly voice. "The fig tree," he says, "shall not bear fruit, and there will not be produce in the vineyards. The labor of the olive tree shall deceive and the fields will not provide food. Sheep will lack pasture, and there will not be oxen in the mangers. I however will exalt in the Lord, and I will rejoice in God my Savior" (Hab 3.17–18).

The prophet denies that the man of God and the worshipper of God are shaken by the threatening events of this world and age, resting as they do on the truth of what they hope, and established on the soundness of their faith. Granted that the vine may fail, and the olive dry up, and the field burn and wither with its grass dying through drought, what matters this to Christians, what to the servants of God whom paradise invites, for whom lie in store all the grace and resources of the heavenly kingdom? They exalt always in the Lord and are joyful, and rejoice in their God, and bear bravely the evils and adversities of the world, while they look forward to good things and future prosperity.

For we have been recreated in the Spirit, having laid aside our earthly birth, and have been reborn. We live no longer for the world but for God. We shall not receive the gifts and promises of God unless we come to God. Nevertheless we intercede and pour forth our prayers that our enemies may be repulsed, and rain showers be granted in response to our petition, and that either adverse events may be removed, or they may be brought under control, as we seek God's pardon and atonement for your peace and safety continually day and night and as we pray insistently.

COMMENTARY CHAPTERS 21–26

Cyprian presents his conclusion that the lack of a common human condition with the pagans (21) is justified in Scripture (22). Repentance remains possible for them (23), which they should accept in view of the reality of heaven and hell (24). Salvation is open to them (25) in response to the promises of Christ (26).

TEXT CHAPTERS 21–26

21. Conclusion (i): We share no common human condition.

Do not accordingly allow anyone to be deceived. Just because we equally possess flesh and body, there cannot be for now any shared agreement[13] between the unholy and ourselves about the nature of the hardships of the present age. We are the worshippers of God, and they are the opponents of God. You should not suppose then that under such a putative agreement you could call into court against us those events that have taken place. It has been foretold beforehand by the prior words of God himself, and by the prophetic witness, that the anger of God would come upon the unrighteous, that the persecutions that injure our human condition would in the future vanish, but also the acts of retribution which have divinely protected us when injured would in the future follow.

22. Conclusion (ii): Scripture prophesies vengeance to come.

How great are those things that, for the moment, are happening here on our behalf. Let one particular event be cited as an example, in order that the anger of God as judge be recognized. It is the day

---

[13]"Shared agreement" is another meaning of *condicio communis*; see previous references in chaps. 8 and 19 and nn. 7 and 12. See also Cyprian *Mort.* 8.

of Judgment, once more, to which I refer, which Holy Scripture announced with the words: "Howl in anguish for the day of the Lord is near, and the crushing judgment from God will come. For behold the day of the Lord comes incurable in its anger and wrath, to make the whole world desolate and to destroy sinners from it" (Is 13.6–9). And again: " 'Behold the day of the Lord comes with fire like an oven, and all of foreign birth and all sinners will be as stubble, and the day as it approaches shall burn them,' says the Lord" (Mal 3.19).

The Lord prophesies that all foreign aliens shall be set on fire and burned to a cinder. This refers to those who are alienated from the divine race and unholy, not reborn spiritually nor made sons of God. For God tells us in another place that they alone will be able to escape who have been reborn and signed with Christ's seal. When sending his angels to devastate the world, and for the destruction of the human race, God issues finally this dire warning with the words: "Go and slay and do not spare on your eyes. Have no pity for the old or young, and kill young women and matrons and small children so that they are completely blotted out. Everyone, however, that has the written mark of the seal on him you shall not touch" (Ezek 9.5–6).

God reveals in another place the true identity of this sign, and in what part of the body it is placed, in the words: "Cross through the midst of Jerusalem and you shall take note of the mark on the foreheads of the men who mourn and lament for the iniquities that are done in the midst of them" (Ezek 9.4). That this mark refers to the suffering and blood of Christ, and that anyone found under this sign is a person that shall be preserved safe and unharmed, is also proven in evidence by the God who says: "The blood will be as a sign for you above the houses in which you shall be, and I will see the blood, and I will protect you, and there will not be upon you the plague of vengeance when I strike the land of Egypt" (Ex 12.13).

What occurred beforehand, when the lamb was slain in a shadow and image, is fulfilled in Christ after the reality that has followed in its place. Just as then, when Egypt was struck, the Jewish population could not escape unless through the blood and sign of the lamb, so also, when the world begins to be laid waste and shaken, only he who is found under the blood and seal of Christ escapes.

23. Conclusion (iii): The disasters are warnings to repent.

Accordingly, look carefully, while there is time, to your true and eternal safety. Since already the end of the world is near, turn your minds to God with dread fear of God. Do not let your impotent and empty despotism over us in our righteousness and meekness give you pleasure in the present age, in view of the fact that even in a field weeds and tares are the despots amidst cultivated and fertile crops.[14] You should not say that evils take place because we do not worship your gods. Rather, you should understand that this is the wrath of God, this is God's testing judgment, that God whose presence is not inferred in his benefits might rather be inferred in his natural disasters.

At least seek God, however late, since already before now God forewarns with the words of exhortation: "Seek God, and your soul shall live" (Amos 5.6). Though you are late, acknowledge God, since Christ also at his coming gives this warning and teaches, saying: "This then is life eternal, that they may acknowledge you the only and true God, and Jesus Christ whom you have sent" (Jn 17.3). Believe in him, who never deceives at all! Believe in him who predicted all these events to come! Believe in him who will give to those who believe in him the reward of life eternal! Believe in him who inflicts eternal punishments on the unbelievers in the fires of Gehenna!

---

[14]The reference here is to Virgil *Georg.* 1.154: "In the midst of the cultivated land, rich in health, the unhappy weeds and sterile tares hold sway."

24. Conclusion (iv): Heaven and hell.

What then will be the glory of faithfulness, what the punishment for faithlessness, when the day of Judgment comes! What will be then the joy of the believers, what the sorrow of the faithless, that they were unwilling here beforehand to believe, and are not able now to return that they might become believers. Gehenna, eternally ablaze, and its punishment devouring with its undying flames, will burn those condemned to it, and there will not be the means by which the torments will be able to have at any time rest or end. Souls will be assigned along with their bodies to excruciating pains, without limit and to their hurt.

We will watch there everlastingly, as spectators in that arena of those who were spectators[15] of us in our time in the arena here. The brief enjoyments of your cruel eyes in the persecutions that you caused will be exchanged for our continuous view of you according to the faith of Holy Scripture which states: "Their worm will not die and their fire will not be put out, and they will be in the view of all flesh" (Is 66.24). And again: "Then the righteous shall stand with great constancy against those who have afflicted them and who have taken away their labors. When they see, they shall be upset with a trembling fear and will be amazed at the suddenness of their unhoped for salvation, saying amongst themselves, having repented and bewailing their anguish of spirit: 'These are those whom we once held in derision, as we made caricatures of them. We had no feeling for their life and we even considered their end as madness and without honor. How are they to be reckoned amongst the sons of God and their destiny amongst their holy ones? Therefore we erred from the way of truth, and the light of righteousness did not shine upon us, and the sun has not risen upon us. We wearied ourselves in the way of iniquity and destruction. We wandered in solitary paths

---

[15]"To watch as a spectator" = *spectare*, refers to Christians exposed to wild beasts in the arena, which did not occur often in Decius' persecution since the aim of the torture was to produce conformity rather than to execute.

difficult to walk, knowing not the way of the Lord. What does pride profit us or what does rejoicing in riches confer upon us? All those things have gone away as though a shadow'" (Wis 5.1–9).

There will be then suffering from punishment without the fruit of repentance, an expression of grief that achieves nothing, and an entreaty without efficacy. Those unwilling to believe in life eternal will believe too late in eternal punishment.

25. Conclusion (v): Salvation.

Make provision, whilst it is granted you, for your safety and for your life. We are presenting to you the saving gift of our heart and counsel. It is unlawful for us to express hatred, and we please God the more in so far as we return no injury for injury. Therefore we exhort you, while there is still the means, while there is still some time left of the present age, that you make atonement to God, and rise from the depths of the shadows of depraved superstition[16] to the clear light of the true worship.

We do not envy you your advantages nor do we hide the divine benefits. We repay your hatred with kindness, and, for the tortures and punishments with which you assail us, we point you to the paths of safety. Believe and live and rejoice with us for eternity, you who have persecuted us for a time. When you have departed thither, there will be there no place for repentance, no enjoyment of an atonement here made. Here life is either lost or retained. Here provision is made for eternal salvation by the worship of God and by the fruition of faith. Nor should anyone be held back, either by their sins or by the years of their age, so that they should not come to take possession of salvation. In this world, for as long as it remains, no act of repentance is too late.

---

[16]"A superstition depraved and immoderate" was Pliny's description of Christianity, *Ep.* 10.96.8: *superstitio prava et immodica*; see also n. 5.

The path of approach to God's pardon remains open and, to those who seek it and understand its truth, access is easy. Though it is at the very exit and sunset of your life that you entreat for your sins, and you call on God who is one and true in confession and by faith, forgiveness is granted to you in response to your confession. Saving pardon is conceded you for your faith from God by his bounden duty as Father, and you pass at the point of death into immortality.

26. Conclusion (vi): The promises of Christ.

Christ imparts this grace, this gift of his mercy he bestows from his subjection to death in the victory of the cross, by his redemption of the believer at the price of his own blood, by his reconciliation of humanity to his God and Father, by his restoration of mortal man to life through being born again from heaven. Let us all follow him, if we can, let us be enrolled as citizens[17] by taking his oath and under his standard.

This is he who opened to us the way of life, he who makes possible our return to paradise, he who leads us to the kingdom of heaven. With him we will live forever, having been made through him sons of God. With him we will rejoice forever, having been restored through his own blood. We will be, as Christians with Christ, at once glorified, blessed from God the Father, rejoicing always in God's sight with an unfailing pleasure, and giving thanks always to God. For no one can be anything other than always joyful and grateful who, though he had been subject to death, has now been made free from its fear in immortality.

---

[17]"To be enrolled as citizens" = *censere,* describing the office of the censor as drawing up the list of citizens and their property holdings.

CHURCH ORDER
AND DISCIPLINE

§1 *The Fallen* (De lapsis)

Preface

This treatise was written, according to *Letter 54.4, on Cyprian's return from hiding and appears to have been his spoken address to the council of African bishops that met at Carthage in late spring AD 251. It should be read in conjunction with Letters 33, 43, 55 and 59.

Cyprian had denied that the certificates (libelli) of the martyrs claiming reconciliation for the apostates could be immediately applied (except in the case of imminent death) without due episcopal scrutiny of individual cases that must await cessation of persecution. This was the first of several councils that were to provide increasingly modified solutions.[1] We see reflected in what he says the various groups to whom he took exception, though he does not mention anyone specifically by name.

Commentary Chapters 1–2

Cyprian begins by declaring the persecution to be at an end and to praise God (1). There then follows (2) a panegyric for the martyrs who had laid down their lives for their faith, and the confessors who had been prepared to do so but had escaped with torture and perhaps a stern warning not to be so obstinate. The latter cases had been very numerous since the purpose of the persecution had been to bring about conformity with Roman discipline and not to punish criminally.[2] Decius had died in battle (AD 251), and though his successor Trebonius Gallus may have initially continued the persecution,

[1]See *Ep.* 55.17.
[2]See above, Introduction §2.1.

it was soon to peter out. Cyprian's image is of an army engaged in spiritual warfare in which Mother Church welcomes a triumphal procession into the heavenly city with each rank and age in the Church duly represented, as a mirror image of an imperial victory procession at Rome.

TEXT CHAPTERS 1–2

1. The persecution has ended and God is to be thanked.

Behold, most beloved brothers, that peace has been restored to the Church and, what of late seemed an impossible difficulty to unbelievers and those of bad faith, our freedom from danger has been recovered with God's aid and retribution. Our hearts return to joy and, with the storm of the deluge and its dark cloud broken up, the calm and serene weather sheds forth beams of sunlight. Praises are to be rendered to God and his benefits, and gifts are to be celebrated with proposals of thanksgiving—although our voice never ceased to give thanks in the persecution.

An enemy cannot be given license to do so much that we who love God with all our heart and soul and ability should not declare his blessing and praises always and everywhere with glory. The day yearned for by the prayers of all has come, and, after the horrendous and monstrous gloom of a long night, the world shines with the rays of the Lord's light.

2. The martyrs' triumphant procession.

We gaze with eyes full of joy upon the confessors, celebrated with a public pronouncement of their fame and made renowned by the merits of the faith. Clinging to them with holy kisses, we embrace the objects of our long desire with an insatiable yearning. The white-robed contingent of the soldiers of Christ is at hand. They shattered the turbulent ferocity of the encroaching persecution by holding their battle line unbroken, prepared for the suffering of prison, armed for the endurance of death. You have offered resistance bravely to the present age, you have provided a glorious gladiatorial performance for God,[3] and you have been an example to the brothers who will follow you.

Your sacred voice has spoken forth Christ, in whom at the same time you have confessed that you had believed. Your hands, glistening in noble purity, had grown accustomed to nothing other than divine works. These hands opposed the sacrifices of sacrilege.[4] Your mouths, sanctified by heavenly nourishment after receiving the body and blood of the Lord, rejected with abhorrence polluting contacts with the relics of dead idols. Your head remained free from the accursed and wicked veil with which the enslaved heads of those who sacrifice there at the Capitol are veiled.[5] Your forehead, pure with the seal of God,[6] could not wear the garland wreath of the Devil,[7] and instead kept itself free for the garland wreath of God.

How does Mother Church welcome you into her glad bosom as you return from the battle! How blessed, how rejoicing does she

[3]"Gladiatorial performance" = *spectaculum* or "spectacle." Here God replaces the Emperor in his box in the arena of martyrdom.

[4]They had refused to sacrifice and to obtain the *libellus,* or certificate, to the effect that they had done so, required by Decius' law. See also chapters 21–26 for what befell those who did sacrifice, or who had obtained a certificate that they had done so, by bribery.

[5]Examples of priests veiled for sacrifices abound, for example, of Augustus; see the Ara Pacis reliefs, or as augur on the Altar of the Lares; see Brent, *Imperial Cult,* 60–63 and plate 7.

[6]The "seal" here refers to baptism, before the fourth century and onwards, when, in the Western Church, the sign of the Cross in oil became associated with a separate rite of Confirmation. See G. W. H. Lampe, *The Seal of the Spirit: A Study in the Doctrine of Baptism and Confirmation in the New Testament and the Fathers* (London: SPCK, 1967), chapter 11, *passim* and p. 289.

[7]*Coronae* of priests decorated with miniature gods and goddesses; laurel wreaths for ordinary worshippers; see also Tertullian *Cor.* 7; cf. Suetonius *Dom.* 4.4, discussed in Brent, *Imperial Cult,* 175–77 ff.

open her gates in order that you may enter in! Your united columns bear your victor's trophies from an enemy put down in defeat. Accompanying the males in their triumph come even females, who have conquered, along with the world, even their own sexual nature. Both virgins are coming by virtue of an act that brings them a second glory,[8] and boys who have surpassed their young years by their acts of courage.

The rest of the multitude of those who stood fast particularly seek your glory, they accompany your footsteps with marks of praise close to and almost joined to your own. Amongst the latter there is even the same integrity of heart, the same wholeness of a faith held fast. The publishing of their names for exile, tortures with which they were threatened, dues paid exacted by law in the form of physical punishment, and property fines, failed to terrorize those resting on the unshaken roots of heavenly precepts and strengthened by the gospel traditions. The day for the examination of their faith was set.[9] But he who remembers that he has renounced the world[10] recognizes no day appointed by this world, nor does a person who hopes for eternity from God now take worldly times into account.

[8]Their first glory is their renunciation of the flesh; the second, the confession of their faith before the magistrate.

[9]That is to say, the day specified in Decius' decree to sacrifice to the gods and receive the *libellus*.

[10]Cyprian here refers to the renunciation of the Devil and all his works in the recitation of the Creed before baptism, as in Pseudo-Hippolytus *Trad. ap.* 21, representing the Roman Church of the second century. See, however, a critical reappraisal of this early historical location for the Creed in C. Markschies, "Wer Schreib die sogennante *Traditio Apostolica*?" in W. Kinzig, C. Markschies, and M. Vinzent, *Tauffragen und Bekenntinis* (Berlin/New York: De Gruyter, 1999), 1–71; cf. P. Bradshaw, M. E. Johnson, and L. E. Phillips, *The Apostolic Tradition: A Commentary* (Minneapolis: Fortress Press, 2002); J. Baldovin, "Hippolytus and the Apostolic Tradition: Recent Research and Commentary," *TS* 64.3 (2003): 520–542; and Stewart-Sykes, *Apostolic Tradition*.

COMMENTARY CHAPTERS 3–4

Cyprian now engages in some clever political footwork (3). The party of Felicissimus, representing the Church of the Martyrs, claimed immediate absolution and accused their opponents of disrespect for the martyrs. Furthermore, fingers were pointed at Cyprian because he had chosen to flee rather than face the magistrate. Cyprian now, with a great rhetorical flourish, claims the highest honor for the martyr, and yet argues that his "cautious withdrawal" was in itself a form of confession of faith. He then (4) professes absolute sympathy with the plight of the fallen, in an effusive description of their grief and despair. Some of the laxist party at the council must have been quite disarmed by this, as if the bishop was going to satisfy what they believed were the demands of Christian love with full absolution. But as Cyprian proceeds, his proposals will hardly satisfy them fully.

TEXT CHAPTERS 3–4

3. Against the spiteful who deny the good faith of cautious withdrawal.

Let no one, brothers, no one disfigure their glory, let no one impair the imperishable resolution of those who still stand firm by spitefully disparaging them. When the day stipulated for them to say "no" had passed, whoever had not made his profession within the time limit had confessed that he was a Christian.[11]

The first title to victory is to confess the Lord when arrested at the hands of the gentiles. The second step to glory is to preserve oneself for the Lord for another day by removing oneself by means

[11]Clearly there was a stated period in the Decian legislation. If the magistrates had not challenged those Christians without certificates to sacrifice in order to obtain one by this time, then clearly they had escaped. Of course Cyprian came into this category having administered his Church from hiding. He was too well known (see Pontius *Vita* 14) to have escaped attention if he had carried on life as normal. Yet, he was open, along with others, to being treated with the "spiteful disparagement (*maligna obtrectatione*)" that he mentions.

of a cautious withdrawal.[12] The former is a public confession, the latter a private one. The former overcomes the judge of this age, the latter, content with God as his own judge, guards the purity of his conscience with the integrity of his heart.

In the former case his courage was quick to respond, in the latter his watchful concern achieved for him immunity from punishment. The former was found ready for reaping when his hour approached. The latter was perhaps delayed, who, forced to give up his inherited property, withdrew for that reason, and not because he was one who intended to deny his faith. He would surely have confessed if he himself also had been under arrest.

4. What Cyprian is about to propose is moved by love for the fallen.

There is one cause for grief that casts its sorry shadow over these heavenly garland wreaths of the martyrs, these spiritual glories of the confessors, these greatest and distinguished acts of courage of the brothers who stood firm.

It is that our violent enemy tore out some of our vital organs wrenched from us by the devastation wrought by his own outrage. What should I do at this point, most beloved brothers? Tossed by different currents of emotion, what should I say or how should I say it? I need tears more than words to express the anguish by means of which I can be able to mourn the blow to our body, by means of which I can express my grief for the loss of a numerous people, once so many and extensive. For who is so hardened and hard hearted, who so forgetful of fraternal charity that he would be able to keep dry eyes? First, he would be overcome by a sudden burst of weeping. Then, standing amongst the many sorts of wreckage of his own

---

[12]Cyprian is here at his most self-justificatory. To argue that as a bishop especially endangered by his high profile he needed to go into hiding to administer and fund a persecuted Church, is one thing; to claim that to have done so is a private confession, second to those who paid the price of their confession, is quite another.

people, he would sob forth with tears that stopped him articulating his words clearly, surrounded by the sorrowful remains that were made unsightly from the extent of their defilement.

I grieve, brothers, I grieve with you. But my very own integrity and my personal moderation does not allow me to sooth seductively my tears when the shepherd is more than wounded himself by the wound of his own flock. I join my heart with each of you, I share the sorrowful weight of your grief just as if I was present at funeral rites. With those who beat their breasts I beat my own, with those who weep I weep, with those who lie prostrate I lie prostrate. My own body parts are struck as well by those darts of our raging enemy, his slashing swords have pierced through my own vital organs. It is not possible for my spirit to have remained unharmed and free from the attack of persecution. My feeling for my brothers who have been laid low has also laid me low.

COMMENTARY CHAPTERS 5–6

Cyprian now switches tack as his laxist hearers wait with bated breath for what his apparent sympathy for their case is really to be worth. He examines the providential reasons for the persecution. The persecution was really God's test to uncover where true discipline had been lost (5).

Moral laxity had taken over and clerical discipline had broken down in the pursuit of worldly business. Christian women had conformed to the dress and ethos of the age, believers had married unbelievers, and so forth (6).

Cyprian here reflects the presuppositions on which Decius' policy of persecution was based, without accepting Decius' conclusions, namely the restoration of an allegedly fallen, ancient Roman discipline in a world in chaos.

TEXT CHAPTERS 5–6

5. Persecution and the moral order.

Nevertheless, most beloved brothers, Truth's account must be balanced. A dangerous persecution, casting its shadowy darkness, ought not so to blind the mind and the senses that nothing of the light and of illumination will remain left. It is only by means of the latter that the divine precepts will be able to be perceived. If the cause of the harm is recognized, the discovery of the remedy for the wound follows. The Lord wished to test his household. Since a long peace had corrupted the moral order divinely delivered to us, the judgment of heaven aroused faith as she lay prostrate and, I would say, almost sleeping. Though we merited more for our sins, the most merciful Lord so kept everything within bounds that all of what has happened seems to be his testing examination of us rather than a persecution.

6. Moral laxity and a lack of faith had led to God testing his people.

Individuals busied themselves with increasing the size of their estate. They forgot both what believers had either previously done under the apostles and what they always ought to do. They brooded over their wealth as its size increased through their insatiable greed. There was no careful respect paid[13] in the performance of priestly rites, there was a lack of good faith in administrations to the poor, there was no compassion in works of mercy, there was no discipline in the practice of morality.

---

[13]"Careful respect paid" = *religio deuota. Religio* here, associated with "priestly rites (*sacerdotia*)," clearly refers to the performance of rites or ceremonies. Cyprian's language shows how closely he was prepared to mirror the language of his pagan contemporaries as he equated the Eucharist with a sacrifice and with a sacrificing priesthood, see *Ep.* 63.

The beard in the case of males was styled degenerately, in the case of females their beauty was artificial: their eyes were given a perversely different appearance,[14] after God had created them,[15] and hair dyed to give a false impression. They were cunning in their deceptions at cheating the hearts of the naïve, they were treacherous in their inclinations with which to beset the brothers. They joined together with unbelievers in the bond of marriage, they prostituted members of the body of Christ to the gentiles. They did not merely take an oath heedlessly, but they even went to the length of perjury. They despised with the arrogance of pride those charged with authority over them, they abused each other with a mouth full of poison. Their disagreements with one another were marked with an intransigent hatred.

Many bishops became administrators of worldly affairs, ceasing their obligation to be to all others an encouragement and an example. They were contemptuous of their divine ministry. Their Chair abandoned, their people deserted, they wandered around the provincial territories of others, and were on the look out for markets in profitable business. While the brothers in the Church went hungry, they wished to hold on to their money in large quantities, to acquire forcibly farms by means of acts of stealth and deceit, to increase their profit by multiplying interest.

What do people such as we were not deserve to suffer for sins of such a kind? God also in his judgment beforehand gave us prior warning with the words: "If they will forsake my law, and in my judgments they will not walk, if they profane my statutes, and will not observe my precepts, I will visit their offences with a rod, and their sins with whips" (Ps 88.31–33).

---

[14]"Given a perversely different appearance" = *adulterati*. For the meaning and significance of *adulterare* as "to counterfeit" as well as "to commit adultery," see *Unit. eccl.* 6 and nn. 10–11.

[15]"God had created them" translates *post manus Dei*, which means literally "after the hands of God."

COMMENTARY CHAPTERS 7–9

Cyprian now describes those who willingly and sometimes eagerly sacrificed (7). He says nothing as yet about those who sacrificed only after being long tortured, though he admits the possibility of such cases. Clearly the latter would weaken his hand against the laxists that he has not yet fully displayed. His thesis throughout is that the persecution was, because of their moral condition, like a medical examination for a disease that had developed.

He describes (8) with great incomprehension a great crowd rushing to the magistrate without even being interrogated, and demanding that they be allowed to sacrifice. In their no doubt confused perspective they may have felt that, despite their Christianity, the social, political, and economic chaos preceding the accession of Decius Trajan required cultic action to obtain metaphysical peace upon nature and society. Decius' sacrament of imperial unity, involving the gods of the Roman state conjoined with the dead and deified emperors, may have had therefore some appeal. The fallen may thus have shared the social psychology of anxiety of their pagan contemporaries.

Finally (9) he mentions the baptised children of believing parents who participated because their parents assisted them and imagines them accusing their parents of denying them their salvation.

TEXT CHAPTERS 7–9

7. That spiritually sick Christians would fall was predicted in Scripture.

We had these events announced and predicted before they came to pass. But we were unmindful of the law that was given and of its observation. We were in this condition on account of our sins. In consequence, because of our contempt for the commandments of the Lord, harsher cures would follow the diagnosis of the condition of our faith in the face of the onset of the disease of our sin. We did not indeed even belatedly turn in fear to the Lord so as to submit bravely

and patiently to God's rebuke and divine examination. In consequence, we did not confront bravely and resolutely both the attack of
the disease, and the examination of our divine Physician.[16]

Immediately at the first words of our menacing enemy a great
number of brothers betrayed their faith. These were not overwhelmed by the attack of the persecution, but they overwhelmed
themselves by falling of their own free choice. I ask you, what act
before unheard, what new event had occurred, that they should go
so hurriedly head over heals to break their oath[17] as Christ's soldiers,
as if the circumstances that they were facing had been unknown
and unexpected? Had not the prophets previously, and the apostles
afterwards, proclaimed these things? Did they not predict, when
filled with the Holy Spirit, the persecution of the righteous and the
injuries always from the gentiles? Does not divine Scripture say,
always fortifying our faith and strengthening the servants of God
with its heavenly voice: "You shall worship the Lord your God and
him alone shall you serve?" (Deut 6.13 [=Mt 4.10; Lk 4.8])

Does it not again say in showing the anger of the divine wrath
and forewarning us with the fear of punishment: "They will adore
those whom their fingers have made, and a mortal man has bowed
down, and a man is humbled to the dust, and I will not release them?"
(Is 2.8) And secondly God speaks, saying: "He who sacrifices to gods
will be destroyed unless it be to the Lord alone" (Ex 22.19[20]). In the

[16]I have translated *probatio* here in the sense of "medical examination," in view
of its association with *correptio* ("onset of, attack of disease") that bears specifically
a medical sense; see Scribonius Largus *Compositiones* 171. Here as an antidote for a
bite from a rabid dog, he prescribes three measures of oil of roses to be used "for that
disease's attack (*in ipsa autem correptione*)." Cyprian's words form part of his general
thesis that the persecution was an examination to secure spiritual health, and those
who had failed the examination needed the remedy of penance. For their soul's health,
this should not be denied them by an easy absolution.

[17]"Soldiers' oath" = *sacramentum*, otherwise used in Cyprian as "rite of admission," if not "sacrament" itself; see Cyprian *Unit. eccl.* 6–7 and n. 13; *Ep.* 63.2–5; 73.5.2
and n. 10; (Firmilian) 75.13.2. Other usages are "solemn oath of agreement or unity"
that keeps individuals within a common society (Cyprian *Ep.* 63.13.3–4 and n. 9);
"vindication of the claim" (75.14.2 and n. 9); "oath in the sense of "promise" or "pledge"
(55.21.1), especially in the case of OT types.

gospel also afterwards did not the Lord previously forewarn about whatever is now occurring and will occur? He was a teacher in his words, a fulfiller in what he did, teaching what should be done, and doing whatever he taught. Did he not determine both eternal punishment to those who deny him, and rewards of salvation for those who confess him?

8. The great crowd of Christians that rushed eagerly to obey the decree.

But what sacrilege now! In the case of some people all these truths escaped their memory. They did not wait to be interrogated and to ascend the Capitol under arrest in order to deny Christ. Many were overcome before the battle, defeated without joining battle. They did not allow themselves only unwillingly to be seen sacrificing to idols. Of their own accord they rushed into the Forum, hastening of their own accord to their death, as if they had ever desired this, as if they were embracing an opportunity being granted for which they had joyfully prayed. How many had to be held there overnight by the magistrates because evening was pressing on, how many even begged that their destruction should not be thus postponed? How can such a person put forward as a defence an irresistible urge as grounds for purging himself of his charge, when he was himself the cause of this urge for his self-destruction? Their steps did not even slip, their gaze become blurred, their vital organs shudder, their arms droop down when of their own accord they went to the Capitol, when on their own initiative they approached to be complicit in the dreadful crime.

Did not their senses become dumb, their tongue stick in their throats, their speech fail? Could the servant of God, who had already renounced the Devil and the present age, stand there and speak and renounce Christ?[18] Was not that altar his funeral pyre, whither

[18]Usually understood as referring to the renouncement of the Devil in the baptismal Creed, but see n. 10 above.

he approached with the intention of dying? Ought he not to have shrunk from and shunned the altar of the Devil, which he witnessed to be smoking with foul stench and smelling of the same, as though it were his funeral rites and the ashes of his life? Why bring a sacrifice with you, you hopeless wretch, why do you place the victim on there with the intention of making atonement for yourself? You yourself are the sacrifice for that altar, you yourself have come as victim. You have burned up your salvation there, you have incinerated your hope, your faith, there in those deadly fires.

9. Baptised infants were betrayed by their parents into losing their salvation.

But for many their own destruction was not enough. The crowd drove themselves to their fatal end with words of mutual encouragement. They hurried on to their eventual dying by drinking a poisoned cup that they shared with other each other. And in order that nothing might be lacking to cap the crime, even infants, placed in their parents' hands or lead that way, lost now as small children what they had acquired in baptism right at the first moment after their birth.[19] Will not the latter, when the Day of Judgment will come, say: "We did nothing, we did not hurry of our own accord to have contacts with things cursed, having abandoned the food and cup of the Lord. The bad faith of another caused our death. We think our parents child murderers. They denied to us the Church as our Mother as well as God as our Father, so that we were trapped by an action for which someone else was responsible because as children, small and unconscious and ignorant of the entire crime, we were joined to a society of criminals through others."

---

[19]Clearly very young infants were baptised in Cyprian's Church, since in *Ep. 64.2.1–4.2 he makes clear that this does not necessarily have to be as late as the eighth day.

Commentary Chapters 10–12

Under guise of a consideration of plea in mitigation for the fallen, Cyprian cannot resist yet another subtle plea for his own self-justification. The only alternative open to the fallen, confiscation of goods and flight would have been the only sufficient substitute to confessorship. Thus Cyprian's own flight is once again justified. He goes on to argue that confiscation and exile are themselves forms of suffering that show the intention to confess Christ, as remaining in place would show intention to deny him (10). Cyprian can then interpret the evangelical demands for self-denial and the rejection of riches specifically in the context of flight and exile in persecution (11). It is the love of money that thus deprives of their salvation those who stay behind and deny Christ in contrast with those who flee (12).

Text Chapters 10–12

10. Flight and confiscation the only real, scriptural alternative to martyrdom.

Nor is there, sadly, any just or serious plea which would excuse the enormity of the offence. One's homeland would have to have been forsaken and the loss of one's inheritance suffered. For which man who is born and dies has not at some time had to forsake his homeland and suffer the loss of his inheritance? Christ would not then be forsaken, the loss of one's salvation and place in eternity would not be feared.

Behold, the Holy Spirit cries through the prophet: "Depart, depart, go out from thence and be unwilling to touch the unclean thing. Go out from the midst of it, be separate you who bear the vessels of the Lord" (Is 52.11). And do not they who are vessels of the Lord and the temple of God go out from the midst and withdraw in order that they are not compelled to touch the unclean thing and be polluted and profaned by the food of death? In another place also a voice is heard from heaven warning what it befits the servants of

God to do and which says: "Depart from her, my people, lest you become a participator in her sins and less you be injured by her plagues" (Rev 18.4).

Someone who leaves and withdraws does not become a participator in sin. It is only the proven partner in the crime that has his feelings wounded by his critics' blows. And for that reason the Lord ordered that one withdraw and flee in the face of persecution, and he taught and acted in order that this might be done. For, granted that the victor's garland descends upon us from the God who counts us worthy, it is nevertheless not possible to receive it unless the hour is come for our garlanding. It is for this time that someone who withdraws for a time waits, if meanwhile abiding in Christ without denying his faith. He who stays behind, however, does fall because his intention in not withdrawing is to deny his faith.[20]

11. Flight in persecution shows self-denial of riches that damn the possessor.

Brothers, Truth cannot make pretence, nor be reticent about the substance nor the cause of our wound. Blind love of their personal property has deceived many. Those tied down by their wealth that was to them like shackles were neither ready nor equipped for withdrawing. Those shackles were the bonds of those who remained, they were the chains that drained moral strength and subdued faith and overcame the mind and placed the soul behind bars. They in consequence, to whom earthly riches clung so tight, became the prey for food of the Serpent who devours the earth in accordance with the sentence of God.[21]

[20]Cyprian does not miss this opportunity for self-justification before the assembled bishops and clergy of the Council of Carthage regarding his own flight at the onset of the persecution; see also chapters 3–4 above.

[21]Thus, he makes it appear as if those who stayed for the persecution and did not flee were more sinful than those who fled.

And for that reason the Lord, master of good possessions and forewarning for the future, says: " If you wish to be perfect, sell all your possessions and give to the poor and you will have a treasure in heaven, and come, follow me" (Mt 19.21; Mk 10.21; Lk 18.22). If the rich were to do this, they would not perish through their riches. Storing away treasure in heaven, they would not have now an enemy and a conqueror at home. Their heart and soul and feeling would be in heaven, if their treasure were in heaven. No one can be overcome by the present age if this present age does not possess the means to overcome him. He would follow the Lord unbound and free, as the apostles, and as many and not a few in subjection to the apostles often did, who, leaving their own possession and parents, clave to the unbreakable ties of Christ's kinship.

12. Slavery to wealth deprives of salvation when the wealthy refuse to flee.

However, how can those held prisoner by the bond of private fortune follow Christ? Or how can they, weighed down with the burdens of worldly desires, seek for heaven and scale the heavenly bodies and their heights? People who believe that they possess wealth are rather possessed by wealth, being slaves to the valuation of their finances.[22] But they are not masters over their money but rather made over and sold to[23] money like its slaves.

The Apostle points to these people who live at this time when he says: "Those however who wish to become rich fall into temptation and traps and many desires and things which harm, which submerge a human being in destruction and ruin. For the root of all evils is greed, which certain seeking have made shipwreck from the faith and have introduced themselves to many sorrows" (1 Tim 6.9–10).

---

[22]"Valuation of their finances" = *census*, or the value of their property determining their rank on the citizen role.

[23]"Made over and sold to" = *mancipare*, used in reference to the legal transaction of making over or selling a slave to a new master.

For what prizes, then, does the Lord invite us to despise private property? With what rewards does he compensate these small and insignificant losses of this present time? "There is no one," he says, "who leaves home or field or parents or brothers or wife or sons on account of the kingdom of God, and he will not only receive sevenfold in this time, but in the age to come, life eternal" (Lk 18.29). Since these things have come to our knowledge and discovery from the truth of the Lord who promises them, not only are we not to fear this kind of loss but rather yearn for it. The Lord himself again proclaims with the admonition: "Blessed will you be when they will persecute you, and will split you up and cast you out, and they will speak evil in vain of your name on account of the Son of Man. Rejoice in that day and exult, for behold your reward is great in the heavens" (Lk 6.20).

Commentary Chapters 13–19

Following his self-justificatory detour, Cyprian now returns to the discussion in order to address to the bishops assembled in council the more difficult case of those who have apostatized unwillingly after considerable suffering. We note how he will use terms suitable in the context of a judicial examination at law, such as:

(i) "Plea in defense" or "plea for immunity" (= *excusatio*),[24]

(ii) "Pardon" (= *uenia*),[25]

(iii) "Case" (= *causa*),[26]

---

[24]Justinian (Ulpian) *Dig.* 27.1.3: "the administration of three guardianships (*tria onera tutelarum*) grants exemption (*dant excusationem*) [from any further such obligation]."

[25]Justinian (Papinian) *Dig.* 50.2.6.3: "those who have abandoned the investigation of a criminal charge without being granted the concession of an amnesty (*qui iudicii publici quaestionem citra ueniam abolitionis deseruerunt*)."

[26]Speaking of a judgment against a buyer who did not appear, an exception is made on a point of law in Justinian (Ulpian) *Dig.* 21.2.55: "He is deemed to have lost because he was not present (*propter absentiam uictus uidetur*), and not because he had a bad case (*quam quod malam causam habuit*)."

(iv) "To forgive a person an offence" or "to pardon" (= *ignoscere*).[27]

Thus he will now consider those who tried to make their confession but were not sufficiently strong to see things through. He speaks first of those like Castus and Aemilius, who went before the magistrate a second time and on this occasion stood firm. Only these can be granted outright a pardon (13).

The vanquished fallen need to provide redemptive suffering compared to theirs even though the persecution is now over. Whether voluntary or under compulsion makes no difference to the need for acts of penance as healing medicine applied by the priest as a physician of souls. The medical imagery in application to the penitential discipline becomes necessary here in order to claim that it is for the penitent's own good that he is not granted quick absolution (14). The principle danger for Cyprian is that they might eat the flesh of Christ in the Eucharist with polluted lips, to their own destruction (15). In reality, the advocacy of absolution without due penance is a new persecution of the Devil, surreptitiously depriving the Church of the benefits of the martyrs (16).

Appeal by the party of the lax to the "certificates of reconciliation (*libelli pacis*)" is vain since it is God, and not the martyrs, who gives absolution. The merits of the martyrs will prevail only on the Day of Judgment (17). Examples from Scripture show that the holiest of figures cannot obtain absolution against God's judgment but only in accord with it (18).

TEXT CHAPTERS 13–19

13. Pleas in mitigation for the fallen: second confession.

"But after the torture racks had come, those who continued resisting were threatened with very serious treatment."[28] So someone who has been overcome by the instruments of torture might possibly

[27]Of a pupil or slave being without blame for the act of a tutor in harming someone, see Justinian (Ulpian) *Dig.* 43.24.11.7: "For an act of harming (*ad noxam*), would not a slave be held innocent (*an ignoscitur seruo*) who obeyed his tutor (*qui obtemperauit tutori*)?"

[28]This was, clearly, one plea at the council, namely that many had lapsed not willingly and gladly but after elaborate tortures had produced unbearable suffering. Cyprian will admit absolution but only after penance, and not immediately, as Felicissimus' party had argued, using these examples as their strongest case.

complain in our Court[29] about those torture racks. He can, in that his pain overcame him, plead the defense (*excusatio*) of acting under duress. Such a person can petition and say: "I wished to join bravely in battle. Mindful of my oath, I took up the arms of allegiance and of faith, but different forms of torture and protracted pain overcame me as I fought at close quarter. My resolution was unshaken and my good faith strong, even when my spirit, long unshaken, had wrestled with the punishment meted out by the torturer.

But I was reduced to exhaustion by the cruelty of one of the harshest of the assessors who resumed again his interrogation. I felt again the lashes of the whip cutting into my flesh. I was beaten with clubs, stretched out on the rack, with pieces torn out of me by the hook. I was scorched in the fire. Thus my physical strength deserted me in my death struggle. The trembling weakness of my vital organs reduced me to inaction. It was not my spirit but my body that failed through what it had to suffer."

Such a plea can quickly proceed to a pardon (*uenia*), a plea of this kind for immunity (*excusatio*) can be treated with compassion. At long last the Lord forgave (*ignouit*) Castus and Aemilius.[30] Thus he restored as victors in the second battle those who had been the vanquished in the first engagement, in order that those who had previously yielded to the fires might be made stronger in the fires. In the place in which they had been overcome they would there in future overcome. They sought pardon, not by seeking pity with their tears but with their wounds, not with a sorrowful voice alone but with the tearing and pain of the body. Their blood oozed forth instead of their crying, and instead of their tears their wounded flesh gushed forth from their scorched organs.

---

[29]"Is permitted in law" is one meaning of *potest*, otherwise generally "is able"; see e.g., Plautus *Rud.* 1329: "*Non potest* (It is not permitted) *triobolum hinc abesse* (to subtract sixpence [from the price])."

[30]See G. Clarke, "Double Trials in the Persecution of Decius," *Historia* 22 (1973): 650–63. Note that at first Cyprian had sided with Novatian's position that only those who wished for absolution could simply make a second confession and be forgiven; see Cyprian *Ep.* 19.2.3, with which cf. *Ep.* 55.3.2–4.3.

14. Penance is the means to find healing through the skills of the priest.

Now indeed what wounds can the vanquished display? Gashes gaping open from vital organs? In the case of some, their physical members did not experience pain as a result of their faith failing in the conflict of battle. Rather the faith was betrayed before the conflict began.

The plea of "crime committed under duress" cannot give exemption on the grounds that they were forced when the crime is voluntary. I am not saying this with the intention of increasing the charges against brothers. Rather I am urging the brothers on to petition the Court that they be allowed to pay their dues for the offence with which they are charged. It is written: "Those who say that you are blessed, lead you into error and they confuse the pathway of your feet" (Is 3.12). He therefore who caresses the sinner with fawning words of flattery, supplies kindling wood for the fires of sin. He is not keeping sins in check but nourishing them. God reproves with stronger counsels, and also instructs, as he induces a brother to look for salvation. "'Those whom I love,' says the Lord, 'I reprove and chastise'" (Rev 3.19).

So ought the priest of the Lord provide healing medicines of salvation instead of leading astray by compliance with their deceitful desires. It is an unskilled doctor who examines the swelling hollows of wounds with a hand that acts sparingly. He only increases the infection shut up within in the deep recesses of the organs while he is trying to preserve them. The wound requires opening up, and being operated on, and receiving treatment with a far stronger remedy that involves the excision of putrefactions. Although his sick patient, lacking endurance in his pain, initially screams and cries out and complains, he afterwards gives thanks when he will experience his health restored.

15. Felicissimus' policy harms those whom it purports in love to benefit.

There has emerged, most beloved brothers, a new kind of injury. Just as if the storm of persecution had raged too little, a deceiving evil and a seductive disease is making its added contribution to the claims mounting up under the label of compassion. It is an unfounded opinion of certain people and is against the validity of the gospel, and against the law of the Lord and of God. Some who are lowering their guard are weakening the bond that binds us in communion. It is an invalid and false reconciliation,[31] dangerous to those who grant it, and liable to be of no advantage to those who receive it.

Their aim is not the patient application required to bring health nor the true remedy that come from making atonement. Any feeling of remorse has been shaken from their hearts, and the conscious memory erased of a most serious and extreme sin. The wounds of the dying are laid open, whose lethal blow, having left its mark deep and profoundly in their vital organs, conceals itself behind a pretended distress. Returning from the altars of the Devil they approach the Sacrament[32] of the Lord with hands filthy and tainted with the roasting smell of the sacrifice.

Now, almost belching forth the taste of the foods of the idols that bring them death, their throats exhale yet more evidence of their wickedness. They smell of what they tasted to their destruction. They are on the point of invading the body of the Lord when divine Scripture resists them and cries out with the words: "Every clean person shall eat the flesh; and whatever soul shall eat of the flesh of the saving sacrifice, that is to say 'of the Lord,' and his uncleanness is still upon him, that soul will perish from his people" (Lev 7.19). Let the Apostle bear witness likewise with his words: "You are not able to drink the cup of the Lord and the cup of daemons, you are

---

[31]"Reconciliation" (= *pax*) usually translated "peace," but here clearly referring to reconciliation by readmission to community.

[32]See also chapter 26 below, n. 52.

not able to communicate with the table of the Lord and the table of daemons" (1 Cor 10.20). The same Apostle uses threatening words that are unyielding and inflexible, and he makes his denunciation of them when he says: "Whoever shall eat the bread or drink the cup in an unworthy fashion will be guilty of the body and blood of the Lord" (1 Cor 11.27).

16. The laxist policy is a second and hidden persecution of the Devil.

By spurning and trampling under foot all these warnings, the laxist party are bringing violence to bear upon the body and blood of the Lord. Thus they now sin far more against the Lord with their hands and mouth than when they denied the Lord. They have made no atonement for their sins. They have not even admitted the charge in confession. Their conscience has not been purified through the sacrifice at the priest's hand. They have not appeased the Lord in his wrath and indignation for their transgression against him. They are thinking that the true reconciliation is the one that certain people hawk about with deceptive assurances.[33]

That is not peace but war. No one separated from the gospel is linked in communion with the Church. Why are they calling injury benefit? Why do they refer to impiety with the term "piety?" Why do they pretend that they are linked in communion with those whose tears of penitence they have cut short. These ought to weep continuously and to ask their Lord's acceptance.[34] They are here to the fallen the kind of thing that a hail storm is to growing crops, that a meteor

---

[33]"Certain people": He is circumspectly referring here to the *libellus pacis* issued by the martyrs some of which had been put up for sale; see Cyprian *Ep.*15.4. Note that his attack upon them here is for the benefit of the Novatians: he wishes to show that he himself is rigorous against such a laxist position, despite what they would claim in accusation.

[34]"Ask their Lord's acceptance" = *rogare*, used to ask an assembly or magistrate for formal approval of some matter; see *CIL* 1.582.23: "*post hanc legem rogatam* (after approval has been sought for this law)."

out of its ordered course is to trees, that a plague stricken wilderness is to cattle, that a raging storm is to ships. They deprive them of the consolation that comes from hope. They pull them up by their roots, they creep serpent-like with their infectious homilies towards making the contact with them that brings death,[35] they crush their ship upon the rocks so that it never reaches harbor.

The homily that trips so easily off the lips does not lead to the grant of reconciliation, but takes it away. It does not grant a share in communion but it blocks the path to salvation. This is another persecution and another testing examination, through which our Enemy, with fine timing, advances on the fallen that he has already assaulted with a clandestine act of plunder. Their cries of regret now die down. Their grief is unheard. The memory of their offence fades away. Their cry from their heart is repressed. The tears from their eyes are blocked. They do not entreat the Lord whom they have deeply offended with a long and full penance, though it is written: "Remember whence you have fallen and perform penance" (Rev 2.5).

17. Even the martyrs cannot grant forgiveness but only God.

Let no one deceive himself, let no one lead himself astray: God alone is able to show compassion. Only he is able to bestow the pardon for our sins that have been committed against *him*, who bore our sins, who suffered for us, whom God delivered up for our sins. A human being is unable to be greater than God, nor is a servant able to remit or grant by his own leniency what has been committed against the Lord as a very serious offence. Do not let this become added to the charge list of one already fallen through ignorance of what was foretold: "Cursed be the man who has hope in man" (Jer 17.5). It is

---

[35]"The contact that brings death" is literally a false restoration to communion that leads to horrendous consequences for the communicant, as he will shortly show in the examples in chaps. 17–18.

the Lord to whom prayers should be said, the Lord who is to be propitiated by the settlement of our account,[36] who has said that he denies him by whom he is denied, who alone received all judgment from the Father.

We believe indeed that the merits of the very many martyrs and the works of the just will prevail before the Judge, but when the Day of Judgment will come, when, following the sunset of this age and world, his people will stand before the judgment seat of Christ.

18. The martyrs are commanded to be patient and respect God's justice.

However, if anyone thinks he can of himself grant to all remission of their sins randomly with excessive and undue haste, he not only gives no advantage to the fallen but he is an obstacle to them.[37] He is daring to rescind the commandments of the Lord. We provoke God's anger when we do not observe the sentence that he has passed, and when we do not think that the Lord's compassion should be first entreated. We despise the Lord in assuming that we have the ability to do this.

Under the altar of God the souls of the slain martyrs cry with a loud voice, saying: "How long, O Lord, holy and true will you not judge and vindicate our blood from those who dwell upon the earth?" (Rev 6.10–11) But as well they are ordered to remain calm and be patient. Does anyone really consider that anyone can be willing to become good following a general absolution of their sins? Would they grant such an absolution against the Lord as judge? Would they

---

[36]"Settlement of our account" = *satisfactio*; see the distinction between a mortgage payment and full settlement of a debt in Justinian (Ulpian) *Dig.* 20.6.6.1: "A creditor who will not simply allow a payment in settlement (*qui non admittit satisfactionem*) but desires full payment (*sed solutionem desiderat*) is not to be blamed (*culpandus non est*)."

[37]See Cyprian (Lucianus) *Ep.* 22.2.1 and 23.

claim that before a martyr has been vindicated by God he can claim to vindicate others? The martyrs are commanding that something be done: Yes, so long as the commands are just, so long as they are legal, so long as the priest of God himself does not do them against God.[38]

19. Moses and other holy men never gained forgiveness for an impenitent people.

Moses also prayed for the sins of the people. However he did not gain the pardon that he had sought: " 'I pray,' he said, 'O Lord, the people have sinned this great offence. And now, if you forgive them their sin, forgive; if, however, not, blot me from the book which you have written.' And the Lord said to Moses: 'If anyone sins before me, I will blot him from my book'" (Ex 32.31–33; 33.11; Deut 5.4; 34.10).

That friend of God, the man who spoke often with the Lord face to face, was unable to obtain what he sought. He did not atone by his plea for a transgression that earned God's wrath. God praises Jeremiah and prophesies, saying: "Before I formed you in the womb I knew you, and before you came forth from between your mother's legs, I sanctified you and I made you a prophet amongst the gentiles" (Jer 1.5). He said to the same prophet, interceding very often and praying: "Do not," he said, "pray for this people, and do not make claims for them in prayer and supplication, since I will not hear them in the time when they shall call upon me, in the time of their affliction" (Jer 7.16, 11.14).

Who is more just than Noah who, when the earth was filled with sins, was alone found just on earth? Who is more glorious than Daniel, who more constant in the steadfastness of his faith for bearing a martyr's witness, more blessed in the esteem that comes from God? He was so many times victor when he engaged with the enemy,

---

[38]Presbyters at Carthage had followed the martyrs' instructions and reconciled the fallen by giving communion; see *Ep.* 16.1.2–2.1.

and survived victorious. Who was more well disposed in his actions than Job, braver in his temptations, more patient in suffering, more humble in fear, more true in faith? Yet God says that he would not even yield to these men if they should make supplication to him.

When the prophet Ezekiel entreated for the sin of the people, he said: "Whatever land shall sin against me so as to sin a sin, I will extend my hand over it, and I will break the staff of bread and I will send famine on the land and I will remove from it man and cattle. And if there will be these three men in the midst of it, Noah and Daniel and Job, they will set free neither sons nor daughters. Only they themselves will be safe" (Ezek 14.13–16). Thus not everything asked for by the petitioner in court is granted in the preliminary hearing, but only that which is mentioned in the final decision of the judge who grants the request. Nor should the judge in this case exercise any privilege for himself, claimed by his own human judgment, unless divine authority[39] should approve.

COMMENTARY CHAPTERS 20–26

Cyprian now addresses the thorny question of the theological justification for absolution by a martyr through a *libellus pacis* to a bishop in order to show there is not divine authority for the laxist position. Christ, if he confesses those who confess him, must also deny those who deny him. The martyrs however are *not* themselves responsible, but the bishop *is*, if he acts on their instruction without applying the penitential discipline. Cyprian here produces he characteristic criticism of martyr absolution veiled behind a rhetoric of praise (20).[40]

Cyprian now returns to the theme of chapter 5 in answer to the objection that God did not intend the persecution, which was no divine test but

---

[39]"Divine authority" = *censura diuina,* or literally "the power of the office of the divine *censor*," with reference to the magistrate who classified citizens and their property and who removed them from the list for debased morals.

[40]See also A. Brent, "Cyprian's Reconstruction of the Martyr Tradition," *JEH* 53.2 (2002): 241–68.

an accident. The persecution was the result of divine Providence upon a Church enfeebled with worldly concerns. Israel's disasters were divine tests according to Scripture (21). In consequence he looks at the character of a fallen Christian in order to show his need for the healing penitence thus exposed by the test that was the persecution. We catch a glimpse here of the often aggressive character of the demands of the fallen for readmission (22). They are refusing medicine (23). Cyprian now introduces some horrendous examples of why such medicine is essential.

Dumbness in one instance and, in another, death from choking was the fate of two amongst the fallen (24). Then follows the example of a small child, left with a nurse, whose parents had fled to exile. The nurse had taken her to the pagan sacrifice and fed her with a portion of bread soaked with sacrificial wine. When subsequently at the Eucharist, the deacon foolishly insisted that she drink the wine of Christ's Blood despite her unwillingness, the result was that she collapsed into convulsions (25). In the case of an older girl who knew what she had done, convulsions occurred resulting in her death. Moreover a laywoman with a box that held the reserved sacrament found that fire came from the inside (26). We are witnessing here an example of reserving the consecrated bread of the Eucharist either for private consumption or protection.[41] Furthermore Cyprian's Christian world mirrors here, as it did in *Demetrian*, the pagan world in which signs and portents appeared in nature to indicate the anger or approval of the gods.

TEXT CHAPTERS 20–26

20. The requirement of the gospel is that Christ denies those who deny him.

In the gospel the Lord speaks, saying: "He who will have confessed me before men, I also will confess him in the presence of my Father who is in heaven; he who however denies me, I also will deny him" (Mt 10.32–33). If he does not deny the person who denies him,

---

[41]For an early example of reserving the Sacrament for the purpose of extended communion see Eusebius *Hist. eccl.* 5.44.1–6.

neither does he confess the person who confesses him. It is not possible for the gospel in part to stand on a sure foundation and in part to waver. Either two given parts together must apply with conviction, or both of them together lose the ability to be true. If those who deny will not be found guilty of a crime, those who confess do not receive the reward of their moral rectitude.

Furthermore, if the faith that overcomes is wreathed with the victor's garland, it is also necessary that bad faith that is overcome should be punished. Thus, if the gospel can be unraveled, the martyrs can gain nothing, but, if the gospel cannot be unraveled, those who become martyrs from what the gospel claims cannot do anything contrary to the gospel. Let no one, most beloved brothers, let no one slander the worthiness of the martyrs. Let no one be the destroyer of their glories and their victor's garlands. Let their reputation for the robustness of their faith remain unimpaired.

The martyr cannot say or do anything against Christ. Their hope and faith and moral strength and glory are all in Christ. In consequence, as the people who themselves have performed the commandments of God, they cannot be responsible for what is done by bishops against the commandment of God.[42] Or who is greater than God, or who more merciful than God in his generosity? Does he wish what God has allowed to happen not to have his intended outcome, or does he think he that he himself would be able to preserve us by his own resources as if God possessed less power than he for his Church's protection?

---

[42]Felicissimus was a deacon, but presumably there were laxist bishops appealing to the authority of the martyrs; see n. 41 above. Here, Cyprian is anxious to separate bishops who acted on the martyrs' instructions. Likewise, he wanted to absolve, from among the martyrs themselves, those he pretends to regard as blameless, in the light of their popular acclaim.

21. The persecution was a providential test not an unplanned accident.

Perhaps these things have happened because God is ignorant of them or they have all come about without his permission! Let divine Scripture teach the untaught and advise the negligent with these words: "Who has given Jacob to be spoiled and Israel to those who plundered him? Is it not God against whom they have sinned and were unwilling to walk in his ways, and not to hear his law and he brought upon them the anger of his fury?" (Is 42.24–25) And in another place Scripture bears witness with the words: "Surely does not the hand of God prevail that he should make them safe, or has he burdened his ear that he should not hear? But your sins create a division between you and God, and, on account of your offences, he turns his face from you lest he should pity you" (Is 59.1–2).

Let us rather consider our offences, reflecting on the hidden aspects of our moral conduct and of our attitude! Let us reflect upon the merits of a becoming aware of them! Let our heart come to a sense of our not having walked in the ways of the Lord, of our so casting aside the law of God that we have never been willing to obey his precepts and his saving admonitions.

22. The character of a Christian fallen in the persecution.

Look at the example of someone whose character remained unaltered by the persecution. What can your only feelings be regarding his goodness? What godly fear did he have, with what good faith can you credit him? He had no dread about God to keep him upright. His haughty and raised neck has remained unbent despite his fall, his attitude of swollen pride and arrogance has not been shattered by his defeat.

Lying prostrate and wounded, he utters threats against those who are still standing and unscathed. Because he should not receive immediately the Body of the Lord with hands of defilement or drink the Blood of the Lord with a mouth that is polluted, he, in his sacrilege, is angry with the priests.[43] And moreover, alas, too much for your rage, O wild one, you are angry with a priest who strives to turn God's anger away from you.

You are threatening a priest who invokes the mercy of God on your behalf. He feels that wound of yours that you did not feel yourself. He sheds the tears on your behalf that no doubt you yourself do not shed. You aggravate further the charge, and you increase it. When you yourself behave irreconcilably towards the bishops and priests of God,[44] do you think that you can make God propitious concerning you?

23. The Scriptures contain the medical instructions for such a condition.

Rather than all this, accept and allow what we say. Why do your deaf ears not hear the saving precepts to which we are exhorting? Why do your blind eyes not see the path to penitence to which we are pointing? Why does your mind, closed and estranged, not grasp the life-giving medicines that we both learn and teach from the heavenly Scriptures? Or if future events should make some less confident because they lack faith in them, then the present ones at least should terrify them.

I will now show you the punishments of those for whose sad decease we are in tears. We can observe these punishments meted out on those who have denied Christ. These cannot even enjoy life

---

[43]On aggressive behavior, see Cyprian *Ep.* 59.17.

[44]"Bishops and priests of God" = *antistites et sacerdotes Dei. Sacerdos* is used of a presbyter as well as a bishop by Cyprian, who clearly implies that the former could offer the Eucharistic sacrifice; see Cyprian *Ep.* 15.1.2. The *antistes* was a pagan high priest who had charge of specified religious rites; see Cicero *Dom.* 104. Note that Celerinus calls Lucianus *antistes et minister* in Cyprian (Celerinus) *Ep.* 21.3.1. For its pagan usage see also Tertullian, e.g., *Cor.* 3.14; *Apol.* 1.1.1; *Nat.* 1.12(1).81.22.

here in this world without punishment, although the day of punishment is yet still to come. Some are punished in the meantime so that the remainder might be suitably directed. The agonies of the few are examples for us all.

24. Dumbness is punishment that fits the crime of denial with the mouth.

One of those who of his own accord ascended the Capitol[45] in order to make his denial became incapable of speech after he had denied Christ. The punishment was derived from the organ of the body from which the crime originated. Thus, not being able to utter the words of prayer to obtain mercy, he would be unable to plead in prayer for pardon.

Another person, a woman, was found standing in the bathhouse. Her sin and its evils had left her with the need to make her way immediately to the baths,[46] her action necessitated by the fact that she had lost the grace of the life-giving laver of baptism. There an unclean spirit took possession of her, and bit her tongue to pieces between her teeth that had either tasted of or spoken wickedness. After she had consumed the food that was accursed,[47] her frenzied lips were turned into the weapons of her own destruction. She herself was thus seen publicly to be her own executioner, and could not have survived for long after this. Racked by the pains to her stomach and vital organs, she expired.

---

[45]Roman Carthage, product of the policy initially by Julius Caesar and continued by Augustus, was as a colony modeled on the city of Rome. Hence the Forum, located on the hill known as the Byrsa, contained along with law courts, shops, baths, a theatre and a proconsul's palace, a Temple that predominated above all others to the Capitoline Triad—Jupiter, Juno, and Minerva—which gave the hill its name (Capitol).

[46]See also Cyprian *Hab. virg.* 19–21.

[47]Not immediately after eating the idol meats, for clearly some time had elapsed for her to reach the baths.

25. The child whose nurse had made her consume the pagan sacrifice.

Hear what happened when I was myself present and a witness.

Some parents resorted to flight in persecution, but in their fear they made ill-advised arrangements. They left their very small daughter behind in the care of a nurse. The child abandoned, the nurse fetched her to the magistrates.[48] Because she was not yet able to eat flesh on account of her age, the nurse was handed bread moistened with neat wine for her. That food itself was the remains from a sacrifice made by those on the way to perdition, in the presence of the image[49] around which the populous were streaming.

The mother afterwards recovered her daughter. But the girl was not able to speak nor to point to the wickedness committed any more than she had previously been able to either understand or prevent its occurrence. Then, through ignorance, a surprise occurred when the mother brought her in with her while we were offering the Eucharistic sacrifice.

Then the little girl, intermingling with the holy faithful,[50] could not stand listening to the prayer of intercession and our prayer of consecration.[51] She began at one time to shake with sobbing, at another to toss about with raging, mental convulsions, just as if her young soul were confessing under compulsion by torture, with what

---

[48]The panel of magistrates set up under the Decian Edict to certify that sacrifice had been made to the gods of the state.

[49]Cyprian says "idol (*idolum*)" disregarding any niceties as to which god the idol was. On the Capitol the idol was that of the Capitoline Triad, but on the coins that of the dead and deified emperors whose images were in a high state of coalescence with the iconography of the gods of the Roman State; see Brent, *Imperial Cult*, 35–38; 170–177; 290–296; 328–330. See also n. 45.

[50]"With the holy faithful" = *cum sanctis*, usually translated "with the saints" but referring here to the holy baptised who participated in the Eucharist, as opposed to the catechumens, who, being prepared for baptism, had withdrawn from the eucharistic celebration. This passage illustrates how the young children of believing parents were both baptised and also included amongst the sanctified (*cum sanctis*), so that they also received communion. For the baptism of infants see n. 19.

[51]"Prayer of intercession" is the meaning of *prex* here, in contrast with *oratio* ("prayer of consecration"), which means the Eucharistic anaphora.

discernment she had been able, her consciousness of what had been done. When, indeed, the ritual of consecration had been carried out, the deacon started offering the chalice to those who were present. When her turn came amongst the others who were receiving, she turned her face away.

With a small child's sensitivity for the sovereign power of God, she shut tight her mouth with lips pressed hard together to decline the chalice. The deacon however persisted and, though she was resisting, poured into her mouth some of the consecrated elements of the Chalice. There then resulted convulsive sobbing and vomiting. The Eucharist could not remain in her body nor even in her polluted mouth. The drink that had been consecrated in the Blood of the Lord was brought up from her body's inner organs.

So great is the might of the Lord, so great his sovereign power. The secret corners in the shadows are uncovered under his shining light. Hidden offences do not escape the notice of a priest of God.

26. Death in convulsions at the Eucharist, and fire from the reserved sacrament.

So much about a very young child who had not yet attained an age for giving verbal expression to an offence that was another's. But indeed there was a girl more advanced in age, and enjoying mature years. She managed to creep in secretly while we were offering the sacrifice. She gained for herself, not food, but the executioner's sword and, just as if imbibing some deadly poison down her throat and into her chest, she began to choke. With her life's breath bubbling away, she came to the point of her final end due to her condition. So, suffering the oppression not now of the persecution, but of her own wicked act, she fell dead quivering and quaking.

The crime committed from a deceitful conscience did not go for long unpunished nor undetected. She who had misled Man now felt the vengeance of God. And when a certain lady tried to open with her shameful hands her box in which was the Lord's sacrament,[52] a fire blazed from it. She was terrified so that she dared not touch it. So also in the case of someone else. A man, also himself stained, dared to receive by stealth his portion with the rest while the priest was celebrating the sacrifice. He was not able to handle lovingly[53] and to consume the Lord's sacrament. He found that he was holding ashes in his opened hands.

By this one example it has been proven that the Lord withdraws when he is denied. Furthermore, simply receiving the sacrament does not bring the benefit that leads to salvation if the recipient is unworthy. The saving grace changed into ashes when its consecrating power has fled away. How many persons daily are filled with unclean spirits, how many are driven senseless to the point of insanity! It is unnecessary to run through the deaths of individuals. Throughout the many sorts of natural disasters spread across the globe the punishment is as varied as the multitude of sinners is numerous.

Let each and every one consider not what another has suffered but what he himself deserves to suffer. No one should believe that he has escaped if for the present moment he has a respite from punishment. You ought rather to be more afraid because God has kept back the anger of his judgment to apply it later for himself.

COMMENTARY CHAPTERS 27–30

Having dealt with those who had directly sacrificed (*sacrificati*), Cyprian now turns to the case against those who had obtained forged certificates (*libellatici*) by bribing the magistrate. Cyprian's accusation is that they have polluted their consciences with a formal declaration that denies Christ (27). Even those who have simply been tempted without yielding to offer a bribe

---

[52]I take it that *sanctum* or "holy thing" means the sacrament here, as in n. 32. It is significant here that we have an example of sacramental reservation, as in Dionysius of Alexandria (= Eusebius *Hist. eccl.* 5.44.1–6).

[53]"To handle lovingly" =*contrectare*, used also for fondling or caressing in Ovid *Ep.* 19.141 and Seneca *Cons.* 1.2.9.

need an act of repentance since inwardly they have felt shame for belonging to Christ (28). Cyprian can therefore exhort generally to acts of penitence (29), whilst criticizing the attitude of heart that thinks that, having fallen, one can simply be self indulgent in feasting and in one's dress (30).

TEXT CHAPTERS 27–30

*27. Those who gave bribes for forged certificates (*libellatici*) are also guilty.*

Nor should they flatter themselves that they have less need to pursue penitence if, even though they have not defiled their hands with the unholy sacrifices, yet they have polluted consciences because of their certificates.[54] A certificate is a formal declaration[55] that one has denied Christ, it is the declaration of an intention[56] of a Christian to reject what he has been. He says in words that he has done what someone else did when he committed it in fact. Though it is written: "You are unable to serve two masters" (Mt 6.24), he has served the master of this world, he has observed his edict, and he has preferred to obey a human empire than God.[57]

---

[54]"Certificates" = *libelli,* which were issued by the commissioners subsequent to offering sacrifice, but which were sometimes obtained by bribery.

[55]"Formal declaration" before a magistrate or official (= *professio*), used in this sense in Justinian (Papinian) *Dig.* 33.8.19: "When a master wished to free his slave (*cum dominus seruum uellet manumittere*), he ordered him to make a formal declaration of the property he had administered as if he could legally have owned it (*professionem edi sibi peculi iussit*), and thus the slave received his freedom (*atque ita seruus libertatem accepit*)."

[56]"Declaration of intention" = *contestatio,* used in this sense in Justinian (Paulus) *Dig.* 50.1.20: "One's official address (*domicilium*) is transferred by actually moving it (*re et facto transfertur*), not by the bare declaration that one intends to do so (*non nuda contestatione*): as we are required to say in those cases against those (*sicut in his exigitur*) who deny that they can be summoned for civic duties because they are resident aliens (*qui negant se posse ad munera ut incolas uocari*)."

[57]Note how this sets Cyprian clearly against the Roman Empire and its sacrament of unity in making offerings to the gods of the state. See further Brent, *Imperial Cult,* 4–11.

It is an open question whether his published admission will bring him lesser disgrace and accusation from men. He will not, however, be able to flee from and avoid God, since the Holy Spirit says in the Psalms: "Your eyes have seen my imperfection and in your book are all things written" (Ps 138.16). Again, "Man looks on the face, God on the heart" (1 Sam 16.7). The Lord himself also warns beforehand and forearms us, saying: "Let all the churches know that I am the searcher of the reins and the heart" (Rev 2.13). He sees the hidden things, he contemplates what is concealed and unseen, nor is anyone able to escape the eyes of God who says: "I am a God who is near and not a God from afar off. If a man be hidden in hidden places, will I not therefore see him?" (Jer 23.23–24) He sees the minds and hearts of individuals and, destined to judge not only regarding deeds but also regarding our words and thoughts, he inspects the minds and wills of us all, formed in the hidden depths of a heart hitherto enclosed against him.

28. Penitence is still required, even for being merely tempted to bribe.

Finally, there is the case of those who, although convicted of no crime of sacrificing or obtaining a certificate, have merely considered this. Then they admit it sorrowfully and simply in the presence of the priests of God and they make confession for the sake of their conscience, and so they lift a weight from their mind. Thus their faith is increased and their fear of God is improved.

They ask for saving medicine for their wounds, though these are little and modest, knowing that it is written: "God is not mocked" (Gal 6.7). God is not able to be mocked nor tricked, or to be deceived by some misleading cleverness. Indeed, a person sins more if he thinks of God in a human fashion and believes that he can avoid the punishment for crime without admitting his crime publicly. Christ in his precepts says: "He who is ashamed of me, the Son of Man will put him to shame" (Mk 8.38; Lk 9.26).

Should he think himself a Christian who is ashamed or frightened about being a Christian? How can he be with Christ who blushes and fears to be associated with Christ? His sin will have clearly been less by not looking upon images and profaning the sanctity of the faith under the mocking eyes of the surrounding public, without defiling his own hands with the sacrifices that bring death, and without staining his lips with food that is cursed. Thus far it will help his case that his offence is minor, but without his conscience being free from guilt.

He can more easily obtain pardon, rather than complete immunity, for his crime. He should not cease from doing penance, and from pleading the mercy of our Lord. The character of the offence might seem less, but failure to pay the fine for it might make its consequences far greater.

29. Exhortation to acts of penitence.

Let each of you confess, I beg you, brothers, his own sin whilst the sinner is still in the world, while he can still be allowed confession, while there is the possibility of making amends, and forgiveness, granted through the priests, is still efficacious with God.

Let us turn to God with our whole heart and, expressing penitence for our sin with true sorrowing, let us plead with God for his mercy. Let us prostrate our soul before him, let us repay our debt with mourning, and let all our hope rest on his support.

God himself tells us in what condition we must entreat: " 'Return,' he says, 'to me with all your heart and at the same time with fasting and weeping and lamentation, and rend your hearts and not your garments'" (Joel 2.12–13). Let us turn again to the Lord with our whole heart. Let us placate his anger, and our offence caused, with fasts, with tears, with lamentations, just as he himself admonishes us.

30. The food and dress of the true penitent.

Take someone who, from the first day of his offence, attended daily
the baths, who has gratified his hunger with sumptuous feasts. Swollen with excessive fat, he belches forth daily his noises of indigestion,
and shares not his food and drink with the poverty of the needy. Are
we to consider that he is lamenting with his whole heart, that he is
entreating the Lord with fasts, with tears, with lamentations?

How can someone who steps around happily and joyfully bewail
his own death? When it is written: "You shall not spoil the appearance of your beard" (Lev 19.27) he combs his beard and adorns his
face. So he is now anxious to give pleasure to anyone who displeases
God.[58] Or does that woman lament and mourn who has the leisure
to clothe herself with the smart appearance of a costly dress, and not
to reflect on the raiment of Christ that she has lost?

She accepts priceless ornaments and elaborate necklaces without
weeping her loss of her divine and heavenly adornment. Though
you wear garments made abroad and silk dresses, you are naked.
Granted you may embellish yourself with golden ornaments and
pearls and jewels, without the beauty of Christ you are disfigured.
Stop dying your hair because now you are in grief. Wash now from
your eyes with your tears the lines of your eyes that you painted with
black eye shadow. If you have lost one of your own dear own through
mortal death, you would mourn sorrowfully and weep. With your
face unmade up, with your dress changed, with your hair unkempt,
with your countenance gloomy, with your mouth long, you would
show signs of your mourning.

You have lost your soul, you poor wretched thing. You survive
here as one spiritually dead, and you have begun as you walk life's
way to carry your own dead corpse. Do you not bitterly lament, do
you not continually mourn, do you not hide yourself away in continuous mourning with the disgrace of what you have committed? Lo

[58]Cyprian *Hab. virg.* 13.

the worse the wounds of sinning are, the greater the offences were. To have sinned, and not to be paying the penalty, to have offended, but not be expressing sorrow for the offences!

COMMENTARY CHAPTERS 31–36

Cyprian now holds out the example of the Three Young Men in Daniel as the model for confession and martyrdom. Even though their conscience was clear, they wore sackcloth for their sins, by contrast with those described previously (31). He now contrasts the penitence of the innocent with the lack of penitence of those who have fallen (32). Self-satisfaction has led them to believe they were restored to communion by joining with Felicissimus' excommunicated group (33). Their false absolution damages the putatively absolved since it blocks the way to an absolution that is real (34). Cyprian can thus argue that penance was required for healing (35), and can exhort to work for the absolution that, though the martyrs sought it for others, only the bishops could grant. (36).

TEXT CHAPTERS 31–36

31. Examples of Ananias, Azariah, and Misahel.

Ananias, Azarias, Misahel, distinguished and splendid boys, did not hold their peace even in the midst of the flames and fires of the blazing furnace, but made their confession to God. Their conscience was clear, because they had so often won God's favour by their obedience to the faith and in holding God in awe. They persisted in their humility and in making atonement to the Lord. They did not fall short in those glorious deeds that witnessed their martyr virtues.[59] Divine Scripture speaks: "Azarias standing," it says, "prayed and opened his

---

[59]"Deeds that witnessed" = *martyria*, which can also mean "tortures" and is here used with a double meaning. The whole phrase could therefore be rendered: "the glorious tortures that tested their courage."

mouth and made confession to God along with his companions in the midst of the fire" (Dan 3.25 LXX).

Daniel, even after the many kinds of favour shown for his good faith and innocence, even after the approval of our Lord often repeated regarding his virtues and praises, strove further with fasts that God should continue to be favorable. He was draped in sackcloth and ashes when he made his sorrowful confession and said: "O Lord, great God and strong and to be feared, who preserves covenant and mercy to those who love you and observe your commandments, we have sinned, we admit our offence, we have been ungodly, we have transgressed and abandoned your precepts and your judgments. We did not listen to your servants the prophets, to the words that they spoke in your name over our kings and all nations and over all the earth. With you, O Lord, with you is justice, with us confusion" (Dan 9.4).

32. The moral qualities of the three young men.

They did these things then because they were gentle, they were plain, and they were innocent in winning the favor of God's grandeur. But they who have now denied their Lord recoil from paying their debts and entreating the Lord. I implore you, brothers, find relief in cures that are healthy, submit to better advice. Join your tears with our tears, unite your grieving with our grief. We challenge you, as we are able to challenge God on your behalf, we direct our own prayers to you with which we pray to God for you that he may have mercy. Perform full penance, show proof of the mourning of a sorrowing and contrite heart.

33. The madness of those seeking absolution without penance.

Let not the thoughtless straying of certain people, or their sense of hollow bewilderment, influence you. Those who persist in such a serious crime are so deeply affected by a blindness of spirit that they are neither aware of their sins nor lament them. This is the greater retribution of God in his wrath, just as it is written: "And God gave them a spirit of being pierced through" (Is 29.10) and again, "They did not receive the love of the truth in order that they might be saved, and therefore God sends upon them the working of error so that they trust in falsehood, in order that all who have not believed in the truth might be judged, but have pleased themselves in their unrighteousness" (2 Thess 2.10–12).

Pleased with themselves but without righteousness, and crazed by the derangement of numbness of a mind that has been pierced with pain, they disregard the precepts of the Lord, they neglect the medicine for their wound. They are unwilling to perform penance. Careless before when they became guilty of the crime, after committing it they became hardened. Formerly they had not stood firm, latterly they would not bend the knee as supplicants. They fell when they ought to have stood firm, they decided to stand firm when they ought to have fallen at God's feet and lain prostrate.

They assumed possession, on their own initiative, of reconciliation though no one granted this to them. Led astray by a false promise, and joined to apostates and people of bad faith, they put error in the place of truth, they consider valid a communion of those who are not in communion. They, who did not trust in God when faced by human opposition, are putting their trust in men.

34. The laxist claim remains potentially more damaging than the persecution.

Shun people of this kind with all your might, avoid those who are inextricably involved in destructive associations. Their message spreads insidiously like some malignant tumor, their meeting for discussion is like a disease that knows no bounds, their poisoned propaganda causes far worse deaths than the persecution itself.

A penance that can effectively atone still remains possible in the latter case, but they who remove penitence from the sentence on the guilty block the way to atoning for their guilt. Thus it happens that, while through the casualness[60] of certain people a false salvation is both offered and believed in, the hope of a true salvation is removed.

35. Penitence as medicine for the soul required by God's duty as father.

But you, brothers, who are moved by your reverence towards God and whose souls are mindful of their sin even though they are ruinously fallen, run over your offences in penitence and in sorrow. Acknowledge to your conscience your most serious crime, open the eyes of your heart to understanding the nature of your offence. Do not despair of the Lord's mercy but do not demand his instant pardon.

God is as much to be feared for the majesty of his justice, though he is forever kind and good with a father's duty of care. Let us shed tears that match the measure of our sin. A deep wound should not

---

[60]"Casualness" = *temeritas,* usually translated "rashness" or "thoughtlessness" but also meaning "absence of design" and, therefore, "randomness," as in Cicero *Nat. d.* 2.56: "In the heaven (*in caelo*) there is neither the absence of fortune nor randomness (*nec fortuna nec temeritas inest*)." Hence the term is used here by Cyprian to characterize the casualness or lack of a physician's planned treatment to cure the sin of apostasy.

be spared a long and careful treatment, penitence should not be less than the sin itself. Do you think that you can suddenly gain the forgiveness of the God whom you have denied with faithless words? You preferred to place your inherited wealth above God,[61] whose temple you have profaned with your unholy defilement. Do you think that he can have mercy upon you whom you said was nothing to you?

You ought to pray and supplicate beyond the call of duty. Pass the day in sorrow, spend the night on watch and with tears, fill every hour with tearful laments, spread yourselves out on the ground and cleave to ashes, roll about in goat's hair and in mourning robes.[62] Do not desire any other clothing after you have lost the raiment of Christ. After receiving the food of the Devil, prefer to fast.

Apply yourself to the works of righteousness by means of which sins are purified, press on constantly with giving alms by means of which souls are freed from death. What the Adversary was trying to carry off, let Christ take back, nor should one's inherited wealth be clung on to nor loved. It was by that wealth you were deceived and overcome. Property must be shunned like an enemy, it must be fled from as one would a highwayman, it must be feared by those who possess it as they would a capital punishment or poison.

What you have left remaining over is only so much benefit to you if it is then used to redeem your offence and guilt. May your good work be instant and bountiful, let your total capital be paid out for the healing of your wound. Let the Lord be our investment, expressed in terms of our wealth and resources, on account of which he will give his judgment regarding us. So faith flourished under the apostles, so the crowd of first believers observed his command-

---

[61]Of course Cyprian in fleeing suffered confiscation of his goods for which he can claim the status of martyrdom, though one group of martyrs may well have disputed this.

[62]"Mourning robes" = *sordes,* usually translated "dirt," "squalor," or "moral turpitude," also has this meaning, as in Fronto *Ad Aurelium* 2: *numquam uoluntarias uerborum sordes induisset.*

ments. They were eager, they were generous, they gave their all to be distributed through the apostles, and they did not have sins of this kind to atone for (Acts 2.44).

36. In Conclusion: Seek absolution through acts of penitence.

If anyone prays with his whole heart, if his voice quivers with the mourning and tears of true repentance, if he thus turns the Lord to pardon his sin through his unceasing works of righteousness, to such a person the Lord is able to grant forgiveness. God extends to such an one his mercy when he says: "When having returned you mourn, then you will be saved and you will know where you have been" (Is 30.15), and again, "'I do not wish the death of him who dies,' says the Lord, 'so much as that he should return and live'" (Ez 18.11, 23, and 32; 33.11). And Joel the prophet declares the fatherly affection of the Lord, when the Lord himself also admonishes: "'Return,' he says, 'unto the Lord your God, since he is compassionate and fatherly and patient and of great mercy, and who deflects the sentence he has demanded for your wickednesses'" (Joel 2.13).

God can grant leniency, he is able to modify his sentence. He is able to pardon the penitent, the performer of good works, the person who makes entreaty. He is able to acknowledge receipt of whatever both the martyrs have sought to obtain for such persons and the bishops have provided.[63] Truly, if anyone moves God by his works to obtain forgiveness, if he should conciliate his anger and the offence that causes his wrath by suing for a just pardon, God grants both the weapons by which he who was once overcome is rearmed,

---

[63]The representatives of Lucianus and the Church of the Martyrs would have hardly have considered the role of the bishops as one of completing absolution rather than of following instructions to reconcile those whom they had absolved. Cyprian is as diplomatic as ever in acknowledging his respect for the martyrs but denying implicitly their ecclesial authority. See A. Brent, "Cyprian's Reconstruction of the Martyr Tradition," *JEH* 53.2 (2002): 241–68, at 48–50 and Cyprian *Ep.* 16.3.1; 27.2.2.

and restores and strengthens his powers by which faith reestablished can be reenergized.

The soldier will rejoin his battle, he will repeat his assault, and he will challenge the enemy, having been made stronger for the battle through his remorse. He who thus has paid his due to God, who has done so in penitence for his sin, who has formed within him by his sorrow for his fall more of courage and of faith than disgrace for his sin, has caught the Lord's ear and receives his aid. He will make the Church glad whom he has so lately made sorrowful, and now will merit not only God's pardon but his victor's garland.

§2 *The Unity of the Catholic Church* (De catholicae ecclesiae unitate)

Preface

According to *Letter 54.4 *Cyprian sent this treatise with* On the Fallen *to the Roman confessors who had made peace with Cornelius. It appears to have been written after the council held at Carthage in late spring* AD 251 *when, with the persecution halted and Cyprian able to return to hiding, the first attempt was made to restore order between the laxist followers of Felicissimus and the Carthaginian Church of the Martyrs, and the rigorist Novatians. His work* On the Fallen, *as we have seen, sought to deal with the laxist followers of Felicissimus, and their demands for the ready absolution offered by African confessors in the form of* libelli pacis *or certificates of peace (or reconciliation).* On Unity *sought to attack the claims of the followers of Novatian, who were opposed to readmitting the fallen even on Cyprian's penitential conditions.*

As with On the Fallen, *this treatise should be read in conjunction with* Letters 33, 43, 55 *and* 59.

These texts and their arguments are critical in view of their later use beyond the immediate issues that are addressed, in particular for the position and authority of the bishop of Rome in conflicts between rival bishops claiming to continue the "true" Church in opposition to one another.

Commentary Chapters 1–3

The Novatianists claimed that they were preserving the holiness of the Church by refusing absolution for the mortal sin of apostasy, and thereby not devaluing the witness of the martyrs. It was Cyprian, according to them, that was too lax and more accommodating to the snares of the Devil. It is fascinating to read, therefore, Cyprian's argumentative *tour de force* in which the Novatianists become Satan's hidden army.

As the agents of schism, they are achieving what the pagan power had failed to achieve (1). Scripture points to a rock on which faith is built. They are disobedient to Christ's commandments, and are thus not building on the secure and firm foundations of his house that is the Church, but they are undermining it (2). Open and published edicts of the pagan power are not the only things to be avoided. Satan, publicly defeated by Christ's coming, is now engaged in a new subterfuge. Having failed to shake by persecution those who had stood firm, he has now introduced into the Church heresy and schism. Novatian and his followers are Satan transformed into an angel of light, and, though appearing to be the agents of Christ, they are in fact those of Antichrist. They need to return to the source and origin of Christian truth (3).

Thus we will be prepared for Chapter 4–5 and the promises to Peter as revealing the divinely appointed constitution for unity in the Church.

Text Chapters 1–3

1. The Serpent, and his craft, is seen in the guise of Novatian puritanism.

Our Lord warns us with the words: "You are the salt of the earth" (Mt 5.13). He commands us to be guileless with a view to being blameless, but also wise with such blamelessness. What else is fitting for us, beloved brothers, other than to take due care and, awake with a trembling heart, both to understand as well as to beware of the artifices of our deceiving Enemy? We who have been clothed with Christ, the Wisdom of God the Father, should not be seen to have less wisdom in the guardianship of our salvation.

For the persecution which rages at Satan's open attack is not our only cause for fear, even when God's servants are thrown in disarray and mortally struck down. Caution comes more easily where the threat is openly publicized, and the spirit is equipped in preparation for the engagement when one's adversary declares himself. Our enemy is more to be feared and treated warily when he creeps up secretly, when assuming deceitfully an image of peace he moves serpent-like, with those hidden approaches from which Satan receives the name of Serpent. That is always his slyness whereby a human being is ensnared, that is his hidden and shadowy means of deception.

Thus Satan has deceived right from the beginning, and, seducing souls with lying words, he deceived those that were green with a trustfulness that was less than careful. Thus, trying to tempt our Lord himself, he made his approach secretly, as if again to surprise and throw off course. However, he was discovered and checked, and thus overthrown when recognized and uncovered.

2. The commands of Christ point to a rock on which faith must stand fast.

An example is then granted to us of how to flee the way of the old Man and to walk in the footsteps of the Christ who conquers. In order that we are not entwined afresh in the snare of death through being careless, but on guard against danger, we should take possession of the immortality that we have received. By what means, however, are we able to take possession of immortality if we fail to observe those commandments of Christ by means of which death is combated and conquered?

Christ himself has instructed with his words: "If you wish to enter life, obey my commandments" (Mt 19.17) and again: "If you do what I command you, I call you then not servants but friends" (Jn 15.14–15). These are the kinds of people then that he calls strong and steadfast, established on a rock with a firm foundation, fastened together with a constancy that is unmovable and unshakeable against all the storms and whirlwinds of this age. Christ says: "He who hears my words and does them, I will liken him to a wise man who built his house upon a rock: the rain descended, the floods approached, the winds came and beat upon that house, and it did not fall, for it was founded upon a rock" (Mt 7.24–25).

Take your stand therefore on his words. Whatever he also has taught and done, we also ought to learn and to do. How can someone who does not do what Christ has ordered him to do say that he believes in Christ? And by what means can he reach the reward of commitment when he does not want to preserve his commitment to what is commanded? Of necessity he must waver and wander and, carried away by a spirit of error, be tossed to and fro just like the dust that the wind blows up. Casually staggering towards salvation does nothing to achieve the end of treading salvation's true path.

3. Satanic angels of light conceal by their alleged purity their true nature.

Public and advertised acts are not the only things to be shunned. There are those acts also which lead astray by the weaving of a clever deceit. Our enemy is very clever and very devious. He was exposed and overthrown by the coming of Christ after his light had come to the pagans and his lamp of salvation had shone upon redeemed humanity. In that light the deaf were allowed to hear of spiritual grace, the blind to open their eyes to God, the sick renew their strength with eternal health, the lame to run into the Church, the dumb to pray with clear voices their prayers of supplication.

Our Satanic enemy, seeing idols forsaken and their pedestals and temples deserted by a people that forsook their faith in them, devised accordingly a new deception in order that, under the label of the name of Christian, he might lead the unwary astray. He devised heresies and schisms by means of which he could undermine the faith, by means of which he could corrupt the truth and tear our unity asunder.

Those whom he could not keep imprisoned in the blindness of their old way of life, he entrapped and beguiled by a new method of deception. He snatched men away from the Church itself. While they thought that they had approached near to the light itself and had escaped the night of this age, Satan spread again another darkness amongst those who took no notice of it. In consequence, while not standing fast on the foundation of the gospel of Christ and the observance of his law, they still call themselves Christians.

Though wandering in the darkness, they conclude that they have the light. Meanwhile the adversary is seducing and deceiving them, who, according to the Apostle's statement, transfigures himself as if an angel of light, and grooms his own as though they were ministers of righteousness, introducing night instead of day, destruction for salvation, hopelessness under the guise of hope, betrayal under the cloak of trust, Antichrist under the name of Christ. As a result, while they lie with words pretending truth, they drain the truth of any effect through their artful contrivance. This is done, my beloved brothers, as long as there is no return to the birthplace of truth, nor is its capital sought, nor is the doctrine of the heavenly Master preserved.[1]

---

[1]"Birth place" translates *origo*, which means literally "beginning," "source," or "origin," though is used in this sense in Justinian (Ulpian) *Dig.* at 50.1.6.3: "The truth of one's place of birth (*ueritas originis*) is not lost (*non amittitur*); neither by the deceit of someone (*nec mendacio dicentis*) who says that he comes (*se esse*) from somewhere not his place of origin (*unde non sit*) is it laid aside (*deponitur*)." See also 48.22.7.10, cf. Tacitus *Ann.* 15.44. "Capital" translates *caput* which means literally "head," though is used of a capital city in, e.g., Cicero *Fam.* 15.4.9; I have translated both in these extended senses in view of "return" which implies physical movement. In so translating, I am not attempting to reinforce any possible papist interpretation of either version of what follows in 4–5. Cyprian need not mean literally Rome as capital of the Empire and of Peter's Chair and birthplace of the Church, but may simply be using general geographical metaphors for the voyage of truth.

Commentary Chapters 4–5

The famous Chapters 4–5 now follow, for which the textual transmission of the manuscripts have preserved two versions that are set out below in parallel columns. Benson argued that the longer, Petrine Version (2) represented a later, Roman (4) reworking of the text in favor of an argument for a papal monarchy.[2] The manuscripts in question however appear to support two originally independent versions. Bévenot convincingly argued that both versions came from the hand of Cyprian, the first at the time of *Letter* 55 and the first publication of the treatise, and the second later, at the time of the dispute with pope Stephen on Baptism, and *Letters* 72–73 written around 256.[3]

In a recent study Hall has argued that Bévenot has dated the second edition too late, and that his location of it in the rebaptism debate is misconceived.[4] In consequence Hall concludes that the collective character of the episcopate in that version points to the council of 15 May 252 as the reason for the revisions to the first version delivered to the council of the previous year. The council of AD 251 according to such a thesis must have been directed against Felicissimus and the laxist party, against whom the prerogatives of the bishop as pastor are asserted. The anti-Novatianist character of the present version thus becomes the product of the second edition that emphasized the collective responsibility of the episcopate against bishops setting up their separate, puritan Church. Such a view depends on the validity of the interpretation that sees the primacy of Peter as simply the primacy of individual bishop over their own diocese.

Benson was undoubtedly engaging, when he wrote his manuscript (in 1896), in interdenominational polemic. The Western, Anglican Church claims to share with the Eastern, Orthodox Church a view of dispersed, episcopal authority for whose authorship Cyprian can be reasonably claimed.

---

[2]E. W. Benson, *Cyprian: His Life, His Times, His Work* (London: Macmillan, 1897).

[3]See above, Introduction §5.3. For full documentation of the textual restoration, see M. Bévenot, *St Cyprian's De Unitate Chap. 4 in the Light of the MSS*, Analecta Gregoriana 11 (Roma, 1937); idem, " 'Primatus Petro datur': St Cyprian on the Papacy," *JTS* 5.1 (1954): 19–35; idem, *The Tradition of Manuscripts: A Study in the Transmission of Cyprian's Treatises* (Oxford: Clarendon Press, 1961).

[4]S. G. Hall, "The Versions of Cyprian's De Unitate, 4–5. Bévenot's dating revisited," *JTS* 55.1 (2004): 138–46.

In the chapters that follow we shall see that Cyprian's view was that, to be a member of the body of Christ, you needed if a layman to be in communion with a priest who, likewise, needed to be in communion with a bishop. It was necessary, however, for individual bishops to be linked in communion with each other, mutually accepting each other in life and in doctrine. If a bishop ceased to be so linked, then another must be consecrated in his place by the remainder, and all laity and clergy commanded to communicate with him alone.

It remains a mute point as to whether Cyprian, in either version, saw the bishop of Rome himself as the successor of Peter, or whether each individual bishop was as it were Peter in his individual diocese.[5] It may claimed in support of Bévenot against Hall that Cyprian's defense of Cornelius lead him to think of Rome as the centre, as it were, of the network of inter-episcopal communion and recognition. Thus all other bishops might be, like the other apostles, "of equal power," nevertheless they should use that power to maintain unity by "sticking fast to the unity with Peter," namely the bishop of Rome. In version 2, the unity with Peter has thus become "unity with the Church." Moreover it is also emphasized that all bishops had the same power as Peter, and that the position of the See of Rome, at least as far as Africa and the West was concerned, was simply the starting point in a series. Rather than those who desert the Chair of Peter, it is now those who resist the Church as a whole that undermine confidence in the faith.

In the context of the baptismal controversy, Stephen was entering a "plea bargain (*praevaricatio*) in bad faith" (5) with the advocates of heresy in allowing the validity of their baptisms, and was thus breaking the unity of the Church.

TEXT CHAPTERS 4–5

4. Christ commands we return to the source of unity, the rock that is Peter.

If anyone would consider and examine my words, he would not need the treatment of an argument at length. The method of proof for

[5]See also Cyprian *Ep.* 33.1.1 and above, Introduction §4.

faith is easy to handle on account of a short-cut[6] to what is the fact. The Lord speaks to Peter: "I tell you that you are Peter, and on that rock I will build my Church, and the gates of the underworld will not prevail against her. I will give to you the keys of the kingdom of heaven, and whatever you will bind upon earth will have been bound even in heaven, and what you will loose upon earth will have been loosed even in heaven" (Mt 16.18–19).

Version 1. The received text.

And the same Jesus after his resurrection said to Peter: "Feed my sheep" (Jn 21.17). Upon him he builds his Church, and to him he hands over in trust his sheep to be fed and, although he might assign to all the apostles equal power, he however established one Chair and ordained by his own authority that Chair as the source of unity and its guiding principle.

The remaining apostles were of necessity that which Peter was, but the first place was granted to Peter and thus one Church was exemplified by one Chair. And all are shepherds but one flock is exemplified which is nurtured by all the apostles in unanimous agreement. Can anyone believe

Version 2. The primacy text.

On one man he builds his Church and, although he assigns to all the apostles after the resurrection equal power with the words: "Just as the Father sends me, also I send you. Receive the Holy Spirit: if you will forgive the sins of anyone, they will be forgiven him; if of anyone you will retain, they will be retained" (Jn 20.21–23) nevertheless, in order that he might reveal their unity, he ordained by his own authority that the source of that same unity should begin from the one who began the series. The remaining apostles were necessarily also that which Peter was, endowed with an equal partnership both of honor and of power, but the starting point

[6]"Shortcut to what is the fact" translates *compendio ueritatis*, which is better than "brief summary of the truth," since the appeal to the promise to Peter of binding and loosing is not to a summary of truth itself but to the means to obtain it.

that he himself sticks fast to the faith without sticking fast to this unity of Peter? Can someone be confident that he himself is in the Church if he deserts the Chair of Peter upon whom the Church is founded?

from which they begin is from their unity with him in order that the Church of Christ might be exemplified as one.

The Holy Spirit, in the role of Christ, draws in allegory this one Church in the Song of Songs with the words: "My dove is one, my perfect one, to her own mother one alone, chosen of she who bore her" (Song 6.9). Can anyone believe that he himself sticks fast to the faith without sticking fast to this unity of the Church? Can someone be confident that he himself is in the Church if he offers resistance to the Church and opposes her?

The blessed Paul teaches this same point and demonstrates the solemn obligation when he says: "there is one body and one Spirit, one hope of your calling, one Lord, one faith, one baptism, one God." (Eph 4.4–6)

5. Collective responsibility of the episcopate.

We, the bishops who preside over the Church, are under the foremost obligation to grasp tightly this unity and to assert

> our title to it, with the object of
> proving that the episcopate in
> itself is one and indivisible. Let
> no one deceive the brotherhood
> with a false impression, let no
> one pervert the truth of faith by
> entering into a plea bargain in
> bad faith.[7]

The episcopate is one, an individual share in which individual bishops hold as owners of a common property.[8] The Church is a unity,

---

[7] Note the legal analogies that make the argument of this paragraph like that which is used in court to presiding magistrates:

  (i) "that we may prove" translates *probemus*, which is used of the production of evidence in the formal phase of legal proceedings in Cicero *De or.* 21.69. Here he uses this term of proving in court.

  (ii) "to assert our title to it" translates *uindicare*, which is used in Pliny *Ep.* 4.12.3 of a case brought to court in which the heirs of a secretary are claiming title to their money in conflict with officials of the state Treasury.

  (iii) "by means of a plea bargain" translates *praevaricatione,* which refers to a deal between prosecution and defense to secure an acquittal at law. Cicero, in *Cael.* 10.24, informs us that Asicius was accused of gaining release through such a process, although Cicero argues that nevertheless he had a strong case.

We have other examples of how, unlike for Tertullian, Irenaeus, or Pseudo-Hippolytus, bishops are not simply entitled to expound the faith as lawful successors to the chair of a teaching school, but rather as a magistrate or advocate making claims about their legal entitlement. See Tertullian *Praescr.* 32.1–6; Irenaeus *Haer.* 3.3.3; Ps.-Hippolytus *Haer.* 1.Pref.6. Cf. Brent, *Hippolytus and the Roman Church in the Third Century*, 129–32; 421–24; 445–53; 506–11; Introduction in Stewart-Sykes, *Apostolic Tradition.*

[8] "... as a common property" = *in solidum*, used in this sense in legal theory; see:

  (i) Justinian *Dig.* 40.12.8.1 (= Ulpian *Edict* 55): "If several persons claim ownership (*uindicant*) of a slave, alleging that he is their common property (*communem*), they will have to be sent to the same judge ... But if each should allege that he is sole (*suum esse in solidum*) and not part owner (*non esse in partem*) the decree of the senate does not apply; nor are conflicting judgments to be feared when each claims what is owned in common for himself (*solidum dominium sibi vindicat*)."

which extends into a plurality by the widespread increase of her fruitfulness. The rays of the sun are many but its light one, and the boughs of a tree many but its trunk is one, established in a root that holds it firm. When from one fountain many streams flow forth, their multiplicity may be seen to be poured forth from the abundance of their overflowing supply.

Granted these are examples of a multiplicity, nevertheless their unity is preserved in their source. Break a ray from the sun's globe, its unity does not suffer from any division of its light. Snap the bough from a tree, what is snapped off will not be able to produce buds. Cut off the stream from the fountain, so cut off it grows dry. Thus also the Church, when the light of the Lord is poured forth, though she sheds her rays of light throughout the whole world, nevertheless the light is one that is spread everywhere, but the unity is not cut off from the body. She extends her boughs into the whole world with an abundance of fruitful growth, she opens wide her streams that flow forth bountifully, nevertheless one is her head and source, and the one Mother is rich with the offspring of her fertility. From her womb we are born, by her milk we are nurtured, by her spirit we are given life.

COMMENTARY CHAPTERS 6–11

Cyprian now makes play on the double meaning of the Latin word *adulterare* that means both to counterfeit and to commit adultery. If there is one Church, the appearance of a second is an act both of counterfeiting and immorality. Unity reflects the life of the godhead as the relationship between Father and Son. This is the Church's "stable foundation" that has already been discussed as the rock of Peter (6).

(ii) Justinian *Dig.* 50.17.141.1 (= Paulus *Edict* 54): "Two people cannot be heirs to the common property of one person (*uni duo pro solido heredes esse non possunt*)."

Cyprian will now give clearer definition to the significance of Christ's undivided tunic with reference to the OT.[9] The event from the Passion is interpreted in the light of the prophetic sign of the dividing of Achias' cloak that signified the division of the two tribes of Israel from the ten. Thus the point can be established that Christ's cloak has a message for the indivisible constitution of the Church (7). The Passover as eaten in a single home thus enables Cyprian to require that Christ's body can only be eaten in the Eucharist within the unity of the Church (8). The dove is a symbol of the Church's peace through the indwelling of the Holy Spirit (9).

He concludes that heresy is not simply the product of poor reasoning but of morally defective thinking (10). That defect is in part the consequence of baptism outside of the unity of the Church that cannot be valid (11). Thus Cyprian's path has begun to lead in the direction of the later controversy with Stephen.

TEXT CHAPTERS 6–11

6. Novatian's counterfeit Church is founded on spiritual adultery.

It is not possible for the bride of Christ to be counterfeited,[10] there has been no tampering with her, and she is chaste. She knows one home, she guards the sanctity of one bedchamber with a chaste

---

[9]For the way in which, in Cyprian's exegesis, the New Testament is curiously fulfilled in the Old rather than vice versa, as usually exegeted; see A. Brent, "Cyprian's Exegesis and Roman Political Rhetoric," in *L'Esegesi dei Padri Latini dale origini a Gregorio Magno*, SE Aug 68 (2000): 145–58.

[10]"To be counterfeited" is one meaning of *adulterari*. In the active tense, *adulterare* means also "to commit adultery," which is how it can be used here too, although, as it is in the passive mood, it would have to mean "defiled by adultery." Similarly "tampered with" translates *incorrupta*, which can also mean "untouched by moral contamination." However, I believe that Cyprian is aware of a subtle play on words here, in which Novatian's sham Church is an attempt to counterfeit the real one. Cyprian will use such language in *Ep.* 55.24.2. The act of counterfeiting can be an act of tampering with and could thus be likened to the destruction of a chaste and virginal body. So, there is a transition from "to be counterfeited," on to "to be tampered with" as a forged banknote, proceeding further "to being deflowered" sexually, and finally to the clearly unambiguous violation of someone who is "chaste." See also Cyprian *Laps.* 6, n. 14.

modesty. She watches over us for God, she seals her sons, to whom she has given birth, for the kingdom. Whoever dissociates himself from the Church is joined to a counterfeit paramour,[11] he is cut off from the promises of Christ, and neither will he who abandons Christ's Church attain to Christ's rewards. He is a foreigner, he is deconsecrated,[12] and he is an enemy. He cannot have God as his Father who does not have the Church as his Mother.

If someone who was outside of the ark of Noah could escape, so could also someone escape who is outside the Church. The Lord warns with the words: "He who is not with me is against me, and he who does not gather with me scatters" (Mt 12.30). He who ruptures Christ's peace and concord acts against Christ. He who gathers elsewhere than in the Church scatters Christ's Church.

The Lord says: "I and my Father are one," and, secondly, it is written concerning Father, Son, and Holy Spirit: "And the three are one" (1 Jn 5.8). No one can believe that this unity that proceeds from the Church's stable foundation by God and that is held together by heavenly rites of initiation[13] can be rent asunder in the Church and split by the schisms that result from the clashing of wills. He who does not hold fast to this unity does not hold fast to the law of God, does not hold fast to the faith of Father and of Son, does not hold fast to life and salvation.

---

[11]"Counterfeit paramour" = *adultera, or,* alternatively, "adulteress." Cf. Theodosian Code 9.22.1: *imitatio soldi,* and noun *adulter,* which is used of a "forger (or counterfeiter = *adulter*) of money (*solidorum*)." See previous note. There appears to be here an allusion to 1 Cor 7.12–14: the principle that unbelieving wives and husbands are sanctified and made part of the body of Christ by virtue of their marital union, but union with a prostitute sunders one's union with the body of Christ (1 Cor 6.16–18).

[12]"Deconsecrated" translated *profanus,* used with this meaning for example in Cicero *Har. resp.* 5.9, in a formula the soothsayers used to interpret a supernatural sign: "Sacred and religious sites (*Loca sacra et religiosa*) are considered to be deconsecrated (*profana haberi*)."

[13]"Rites of initiation," translates *sacramenta,* which may also mean "sacraments." I have followed here the root meaning of *sacramentum* as a soldier's "oath" of admission to an army; see also Cyprian *Laps.* 7 and n. 17; *Ep.* 63.13.5, n. 9. For *sacramentum* specifically as "rite of admission," see Cyprian *Ep.* 73.5.2, n. 10.

7. Unity of Israel and the undivided cloak of Christ as images of the Church.

This pledge of unity, this bond of a concord that is held together in a way that cannot be split into individual links is demonstrated in the gospel. The tunic of our Lord Jesus Christ was not divided at all nor torn in half while they were casting lots for Christ's tunic. This indicates that when someone would be clothed with Christ, he receives a perfect suit of clothing, and an undamaged tunic. But what comes into his possession is common property.

Divine Scripture speaks these words: "Regarding the tunic, however, since regarding the upper part it was not stitched together but woven without seam, they said to one another: 'Let us not tear it apart but let us cast lots for it whose it might be'" (Jn 19.23–24). Christ was wearing the unity that proceeds "from the upper part" (that means "proceeding from heaven and from the Father"), which could never at all be torn apart by him who receives and possesses it, but rather with it secures for himself something that has a firm integrity. He who rends and splits Christ's Church cannot possess Christ's robe.

Consider finally to the contrary that someone can make a division. When, on Solomon's death, his kingdom and his people were rent asunder, Achias the prophet confronted King Jeroboam in the plain. He cut his cloak into twelve pieces, saying: "Take for yourself ten pieces since the Lord says this: 'Behold, I tear asunder the kingdom from the hand of Solomon, and I give to you ten scepters, and two scepters will left for him on account of my servant David, and on account of Jerusalem, the city that I have chosen to set my name there'" (1 Kgs 11.31–32 and 36).

Since the twelve tribes of Israel were being torn apart, the prophet Achias cut in two his own cloak. So truly because Christ's people cannot be torn apart, his tunic, "woven without seam," and holding fast together, has not become divided amongst its owners. The description "unable to be split (united, linked together),"[14] reveals the concord that holds together the unity of our people who have put on Christ. By the sign and seal of the tunic Christ has declared the unity of his Church.

8. The Passover completes the Eucharist within the one Church.

Who therefore is so heinously criminal and marked by treachery, who so wild with the frenzy of discord, that he either believes that the Lord's robe, Christ's Church, can be torn asunder, or dares in fact so to tear apart the unity of God? Christ himself in his gospel warns and teaches, saying: "And there will be one Flock and one Shepherd" (Jn 10.16). Does anyone consider that there is able to be in one place either many pastors or many flocks?[15]

The Apostle Paul, instilling this selfsame unity in us, beseeches and exhorts with the words: "I beseech you brothers," he claims, "in the name of our Lord Jesus Christ, that you keep on speaking to the same end, and that there be not schisms amongst you, be instead reconciled in the same mind and in the same opinion," (1 Cor 1.10) and secondly he says, "sustaining one another in love, acting suf-

[14]"Unable to be split," translated *indiuiduus*, literally means "indivisible," but is a good word for Cyprian's purpose since it is used for "atom" in Democritus and others, as in the definition *indiuiduum corpus* (= "body unable to be split") in Cicero *Fin.* 1.17.

[15]Cyprian here as elsewhere considers that ecclesiastical authority is, like that of a Roman magistrate who has *imperium*, exercised within a spatial, geographical boundary duly sacralized as when the *pomerium* or city boundary is cleansed by the *suovetaurilia*; see Brent, *Imperial Cult*, 83–88. The Roman community, some sixteen years previously, had consisted of a collection of house-churches in a loose confederation with a presiding presbyter bishop; see Brent, *Hippolytus*, 398–406; Stewart-Sykes, *Apostolic Tradition*, 12–16. If one's model is of a philosophical school, then there can be a plurality of teachers. Tertullian, in *Praescr.* 32, for example, sees the apostles and their associates as such a plurality between whose teaching there may be a "family resemblance," *consanguinitas,* and not strict equivalence. Cyprian's church constitution is one of a political state, which must possess equivalent laws and judicial acts. See also above, Introduction §3.

ficiently to preserve the unity of the Spirit in the joining together in peace" (Eph 4.2–3). Do you think that you will be able to stand fast and to live, whilst you withdraw from the Church, setting up the foundations of other Chairs, and different places of abode, when it is said to her in whom the Church is prefigured: "You shall gather your father and your mother and your brothers and the whole house of your father in your own house. And it will be that all who leave the gate of your house will bear their own guilt" (Josh 2.18–19).

Likewise, does the rite of the Passover comprise anything else in the law of Exodus than that the lamb, who is slain as a type of Christ, should be eaten in one house? God speaks, saying: "in one house shall it be consumed: you shall not throw the flesh out of doors from your house" (Ex 12.46). It is not possible to throw the flesh of Christ and the Lord's holy sacrament out of doors, neither is there any other home for those who believe except the Church. The Holy Spirit in the Psalms denotes this home as the accommodation of unity of purpose, and proclaims, saying: "God who makes men dwell in one mind in one house" (Ps 67.7). In the house of God, in the Church of Christ, those of one mind dwell, they continue in concord and pure simplicity.

9. The dove as the symbol of the indwelling of the Holy Spirit in the Church.

For this reason the Holy Spirit came in the form of a dove. The dove is a purely simple and joyful living creature. It is not venomously bitter, it does not bite savagely, its claws do not slash with violence, it loves human entertainment, it enjoys the experience of one home. When they give birth they bring forth their offspring together, when they travel around in flight they flock together. They spend their life in sociable mutual association. They recognize the concord of peace in the kiss of the beak. They fulfill the law of being in one mind about all things.

This is the pure simplicity to be experienced in the Church, this is the divine affection that is to be attained, so that love for the brotherhood might imitate doves, that clemency and gentleness may equal that of lambs and sheep. What business in the Christian's heart has the wildness of wolves and the savagery of dogs, and the deadly poison of snakes, and the bloody cruelty of wild beasts? It is cause for thanksgiving when such persons as these are excluded from the Church in order that they might not take as plunder the doves, Christ's sheep, by their cruel and poisonous contact.

Bitterness cannot grow together and be joined with sweetness, darkness with light, storms with fine weather, war with peace, barrenness with fruitfulness, drought with springing wells, a storm with a calm. Let no one think that good men can withdraw from the Church. The wind does not sweep away the wheat crop, nor does a storm rip up a tree established by a firm root. The empty chaff are tossed about by the storm, sick trees are knocked over by the onset of the gale. John the Apostle abhors these men and lands them a blow when he says: "They went out from us but they were not of us; for if they had been of us, they would have remained with us" (1 Jn 2.19).

10. Heresies reflect the moral character of their adherents.

For this reason heresies both have been committed and continue being committed, because a mind that is perverted does not have peace, because bad faith that causes discord does not maintain unity. Indeed the Lord allows these things to occur and endures them. He permits to remain the natural exercise of free will, in order that, while his discernment of the truth examines our hearts and minds, the pure faith of those that are approved might become clear as his light reveals it.

The Holy Spirit through the Apostle forewarns with the words: "There ought to be heresies in order that the approved might be manifested amongst you" (1 Cor 11.19). Thus is the approval of the faithful tested, thus are those of bad faith uncovered, thus even before the Day of Judgment here also already are the souls of the just and the unjust separated, and the chaff divided from the wheat. The latter are those who give themselves precedence, by their own initiative, in ill-considered conventicles, without divine due order, who put themselves in supreme charge without any law of appointment, who, when no one grants them the episcopate, take on for themselves the bishop's name.

The Holy Spirit in the Psalms indicates those who are "seated on a chair of the plague" (Ps 1.1). They are instruments of the plague that corrupts faith, serpents deceiving with their tongue, and master-craftsmen at corrupting the truth, spewing forth from their infectious tongues their lethal poisons. Their speech twists serpent-like as a malignant disease, whose progress in the breasts and in the hearts of individual patients infuses its deadly secretion.

11. Baptism given in heresy has no efficacy.

The Lord reigns back his errant people and recalls them from these kinds of heretic. This is his proclamation against their like: "Do not listen to the speeches of the false prophets, since the visions of their hearts frustrate them. They talk, but not from the mouth of the Lord. They speak to those who reject the word of the Lord: 'There will be peace for you and for all who walk in their own desires.' To everyone who walks in the error of his own heart: 'Evils will not come upon you.' I have not spoken to them, and they themselves prophesy falsely. If they had stood in my counsel and had heard my words, and if they had taught my people, they would have turned them from their evil thoughts" (Jer 23.16–17).

The Lord again points out and makes reference to these same people when he says: "They have abandoned me, the fountain of living water, and have dug for themselves ruined cisterns which cannot hold water" (Jer 23.21–22). When there cannot be another baptism besides the indivisible one, they think that they are able to baptise.[16] Having forsaken the font of life, they are promising the grace of the water of life and of salvation. These men are not cleansed but rather are soiled, their sins are not purified but, more correctly, piled high. That giving of birth does not produce sons for God but for the Devil. Having been born through a lie, they cannot take possession of the promises of truth, having been conceived from an act of bad faith, they lose faith's gracious gift. They cannot attain to the reward of the peace of being reconciled, who by their wild excitement for discord have fractured the peace.

Commentary Chapters 12–16

Cyprian now considers the counter argument from Scripture of those who would constitute the Church purely on the authority of a self-gathered community. He argues that Christ by "two or three are gathered," means gathered in the unity of the Church and not against it in separation (12).

Christ's requirement to forgive before offering sacrifice condemns them (13). Martyrdom in schism cannot be efficacious since in separating the schismatic does not practice the commandment of love (14). They work miracles only apparently in Christ's name, in fulfillment of Christ's prediction of the false prophets at the end of the age (15–16).

Text Chapters 12–16

12. A false interpretation of the Church gathered as "two or three."

There are some people who would deceive themselves with a quite baseless interpretation of when the Lord said: "Wherever two or

---

[16]This sentence is critical evidence that Cyprian is addressing the rigorist Novatians and not the laxist followers of Felicissimus here. The former were rebaptizing those whom Cyprian's church had baptised; see Cyprian *Ep.* 73.2.1.

three are gathered in my name, I am with them" (Mt 18.20).[17] They should not! They are corrupters of the gospel who put forward these words at a passage's end, but pass over what is just above them. They bring part to our attention, but cunningly suppress part.

They cut off this sentence from its context in the whole paragraph just and precisely because the Church has cut *them* off. For our Lord, when he was urging his disciples to dwell in unity and peace, said: "I say to you, if there is agreement by two of you on earth concerning anything that you ask of my Father, it shall be granted you by my Father who is in heaven. Wherever two or three are gathered in my name, I am with them" (Mt 18.19–20) showing that the greatest value is assigned not to any great number of those who pray but to their unanimous agreement.

Jesus says: "If two of you shall agree on earth." He placed unanimous agreement first but his prior assumption is the concord of peace. He taught that we should come faithfully and firmly to agreement. How then is it possible for him to come to an agreement with someone who does not agree with the body of the Church itself, with the universal brotherhood? How can two or three be gathered in the name of Christ when they are resolved to separate from Christ and from his gospel?

The fact is that we did not withdraw from them but they from us.[18] They forsook the fountainhead and source of the truth by

---

[17]Cyprian's argument here has been cited in order to show that it is Felicissimus and the laxist party against whom this treatise is directed: Novatian would not have claimed that two or three could decide to set up a Church outside of episcopal order on the grounds of Christ's words. But, neither would the laxists, who nevertheless claimed the order of the Church of the martyrs. It is difficult to determine what particular organized group would have claimed such a justification. Some Novatianists might claim that the godly agreement of a few to set up a rival bishop was justified on the grounds of the Church's purity. It might also be an argument of some people who sought to avoid the question of rightful order, perhaps with a view to being nonjudgmental on any side: Christians do not always feel the need to commit themselves to one or other group in a conflict.

[18]Novatian withdrew on the grounds of the error of the Catholic Church, but this can hardly apply to Felicissimus' group, who rather were expelled.

giving birth to heresies and schisms in the process of establishing for themselves different places of association apart from us. The Lord however is speaking of his own Church, and he is speaking to those who are in the Church. His condition is that, granted they are but two or three, they themselves should be of one mind. According to that which he commanded and admonished, granted that two or three were gathered and prayed with unanimous agreement, they are able to bring to pass that which they claim of the majesty of God. "Wherever there are two or three," he says, "I am with them." With those of holy simplicity of course, and those who are at peace, with those who fear God and observe the precepts of God. I agree only that he claims to be with *these* two or three. In this way he was also with the three boys in the furnace of fire: because they remained in holy simplicity towards God and in one mind amongst themselves, God kept them alive with the breath of refreshing dew as they passed through the midst of the flames that surrounded them (Dan 3.49 LXX). In this same way he himself was also with the two apostles shut up in jail (Acts 5.19–21): because of their holy simplicity and being in one mind, he himself with the bolts of the prison released, set them again in the market place in order that they might deliver the word that they used faithfully to preach to the multitude. When, therefore, he who founded and created the Church lays it down in his precepts with the words: "Where there are two or three, I am with them," he does not distinguish these persons *from* the Church. Rather he censures those of bad faith for their discord and commends with his own voice those of true faith for their peace. Christ reveals that he himself is rather *with* the two or three praying together with one mind than *with* the majority who are disagreeing, and that more can be granted by the harmonious prayer of the few than by the discordant praying of the many.

13. Christ's law condemns the irreconcilable heretic.

For that reason also, when Christ gives the law of prayer, he adds the words: "When you will stand up to pray, forgive if you have anything against anyone, in order that also your Father who is in heaven may forgive you your sins" (Mt 5.23–24). He recalls from the altar him who was approaching the sacrifice with conflict in his heart, and orders him first to agree together with his brother, and then to return with peace to offer his gift to God. Neither in Cain's case did God respect his offerings, for neither was Cain able to propitiate God when he did not, through the jealousy responsible for the discord, have peace with his brother.

To what peace, therefore, do the enemies of the brothers pledge themselves? What sacrifices do the imitators of the priests believe that they themselves celebrate? Do they who are gathered together *outside* Christ's Church think that Christ is with them when they have thus gathered together?

14. Martyrdom cannot atone for schism, where love is absent.

Such persons, even if they have been slain whilst confessing the name, their stains will not be washed away with their blood.[19] The blame for discord is serious and cannot be atoned for, and is not purified through suffering. Someone not in the Church cannot be a martyr.[20] Someone who has abandoned the Church that is destined to reign will not be able to arrive at the kingdom of heaven.

[19]Such criticisms would work as well again Felicissimus as well as Novatian, both of whom claimed in different ways that martyrdom made their faction legitimate, and that Cyprian was devaluing what the confessors had gained for the Church; see also following note.

[20]Cyprian here is developing new principles. There are features of the tradition that he dare not explore without injuring his case. Ps.-Hippolytus *Trad. ap.* 9 makes it clear that not only martyrdom as baptism in blood goes proxy for one's baptism in water, but also one can act as priest or deacon without the imposition of hands. Cyprian is here denying a self-authenticating ministry with a long history in the tradition; see A. Brent, "Cyprian and the question of *ordinatio per confessionem*," StPatr

Christ gave to us his peace, he instructed us to be in concord and of one mind, and he committed to our trust the unimpaired and inviolate binding covenants of Christian love. He is unable to display himself as a martyr who has not held fast to love for the brotherhood. The Apostle Paul teaches this, and adds his words of witness: "And if I should have faith so that I should remove mountains, but have not love, I am nothing. And if I should distribute all my goods for food, and if I should hand over my body in order that I should burn, but not have love, I profit nothing. Love is generous hearted, love is kindly, love does not engage in rivalry, is not puffed up, is not enraged, does not behave wrongly, does not think evil; it delights in all things, it believes all things, it hopes all things, it bears all things; love never fails" (1 Cor 13.2–8).

Paul says that "never does love fail." There will always be love in the kingdom, love will endure for eternity, with the unity of the brotherhood remaining rooted in it. Discord cannot attain the kingdom of heaven. He who has violated the love of Christ by the treachery of disunion will not be able to continue through to the reward of the Christ who said: "This is my commandment, that you love one another in the way in which I have loved you" (Jn 15.12). He who does not have love does not have God. Hear John the blessed Apostle: "God," he says, "is love, and he who abides in God abides in love and God abides in him" (1 Jn 4.16).

Those who are unwilling to be of one mind in the Church of God are unable to abide with God. Even though they burn in the flames, and, surrendered to the fire, or exposed to the wild beasts, they should lay down their lives, the latter will not be their crown of faith but the punishment of their bad faith. Their death will enjoy no renown for its religious courage but an annihilation of despair. Such a person can be slain, he cannot be crowned.[21]

36 (2001):327–32; idem, "Cyprian's Reconstruction of the Martyr Tradition," *JEH* 53.2 (2002): 251–263.

[21]Once again the implication of Cyprian's argument is that martyrdom gives no self-authenticating ecclesial authority, since it depends for its validity on a valid ecclesiastical hierarchy; see also previous note.

Thus he professes himself to be a Christian in the manner in which the Devil also often lied that he was Christ, as the Lord forewarned and said: "Many will come in my name saying: 'I am the Christ,' and will deceive many" (Mt 24.5). Just as the latter is not Christ even though he deceives in his name, so also neither can someone be regarded as a Christian when he does not abide in the truth of his gospel and faith.

15. Even deceivers will practice miracles, as Christ warned.

It is both sublime and awe-inspiring to prophesy as well as to expel daemons and to perform great supernatural acts of power on earth. But someone found preoccupied in all such things does not by them gain the celestial kingdom unless he walks by carefully tracing the right path. The Lord voices the words of his authority: "Many will say to me in that day, 'Lord, Lord, have we not prophesied in your name and in your name expelled the daemons, and in your name exercised miraculous powers?' And then I shall say to them: 'I never knew you, depart from me you who work injustice'" (Mt 7.22–23).

Justice is necessary for anyone to be able to win the favor of God as his judge. The Lord in the gospel, when he in a briefly expressed summary directs our path to hope and faith, says: "'The Lord your God is one God, and you shall love the Lord your God with your whole heart and with your whole soul and with your whole strength.' This is the first and the second is like it: 'You shall love your neighbor as yourself.' On these two precepts hang the whole law and the prophets" (Mt 22.40). He taught unity and love together in what his teaching directs: he brought together all the Prophets and the Law in these two precepts.

What unity does someone preserve, what love does he guard or have in mind, who, wild with the frenzy of discord, rends the Church asunder, destroys the faith, disturbs the peace, throws love away, profanes his solemn obligation?

16. Christ prophesies of the end of the age and present events.

This evil, most faithful brothers, began even in past time, but now the same evil grows in size to threatening proportions of destructiveness. It is a poisonous disease that begins to rise up and spring forth, wrought by heretical perversity and by schisms, even as ought to happen at the world's sunset.[22] The Holy Spirit through the Apostle forewarned with this prediction: "In the last days, distressing times will come; there will be men pleasing themselves, proud, puffed up, covetous, blasphemers, refusing to listen to their parents, ungrateful, irreligious, without favorable disposition, without covenant, false accusers, without self-control, harsh, not loving good, betrayers, insolent, inflated with lust, loving their own base desires more than God, having a perverted form of religion but denying its power. From amongst these are those who slink into homes, and take as their trophies little hussies laden with their sins, who are led by all kinds of desires, always teaching and never reaching the knowledge of the truth. And in the way in which Jamnes and Mambres resisted Moses, so all these resist the truth. But they will not progress very much for their ignorance will be manifest to all, just as in the case of the former" (2 Tim 3.1–9).

Whatever words were said beforehand are being fulfilled, and, with the end of the age drawing near, they will come to pass as men are searched and examined along with the times. With our adversary venting his rage more and more, error deceives, stupidity leads astray, envy kindles, passion makes blind, impiety perverts, pride puffs up, discord disturbs, and wrath is hasty.

[22]"At the world's sunset" = *in occasu mundi*. Cyprian shares with his pagan contemporaries the belief that both nature and society is the last phase of its decline, that the world has reached "old age" (*senectudo mundi*). On the pagan side, this received justification from a cyclic view of history in which ages of gold, bronze, and iron succeeded one another and returned, supported by a Stoic eschatology in which all things returned to the primal fire and were reborn. Cyprian will see both the moral corruption and dissension of pagan society and divisions within the Church along with heretical corruption of doctrine as indicative of that End, which would involve the Second Advent of Christ; see Introduction, §2.1, Cyprian *Don.* 14–16 and *Demetr.* 3–4.

COMMENTARY CHAPTERS 17–19

Since Christ predicted the great deception of heretics, we can recognise its corruption now that it is present. Those in revolt against God's sacred bishops cannot succeed in offering a valid sacrifice, and are therefore desecrators of the Eucharist (17). Cyprian equates the OT sacerdotal system with that of the Christian priesthood. Thus he can place the Novatians in the same category of Core, Dathan, and Abiron, who offered such invalid sacrifices, or for that matter, king Ozias who became leprous when he tried to act as a priest (18). They are in a worse condition than the fallen in persecution since the former can atone by reversing their denial through successful martyrdom, but the Novatians cannot become true martyrs if they suffer in separation from the Church (19).

TEXT CHAPTERS 17–19

17. Novatian is erecting a rival altar in rebellion against the true episcopate.

Let not the overwhelming outbreak of treachery move or disturb us, but rather let it invigorate our faith by the truth of what was announced beforehand. Just as some have started to become these kinds of people because these things were predicted beforehand, so the rest of the brothers should beware of these kinds of people. These things were predicted before, with the Lord setting it out and saying: "You however beware: behold I have predicted all things to you" (Mk 13.23).

Avoid, I beg of you, men of this kind, and keep distant from your flank and from your ears their destructive communications, as you would contact with a contagious death. As it is written: "Hedge in your ears with thorns and be unwilling to hear a wicked tongue" (Sir 28.28), and again: "The worst conversations corrupt good characters" (1 Cor 15.33). The Lord teaches and advises us to withdraw from such people. "They are blind," he says, "leaders of the blind:

however, a blind man leading a blind man falls into the same ditch" (Mt 15.14). Such a person who has separated from the Church should be avoided and shunned.

A man of this sort has changed direction and sins, and he is condemned by his very self. Or does someone who works against Christ's priests, who dissociates himself from the community of his clergy and people, think to himself to be with Christ? He is bearing arms against the Church, he is offering resistance to God's ordered arrangement. An enemy of the altar, a rebel against Christ's sacrifice, of bad faith instead of faithfulness, guilty of sacrilege instead of proper religious practice, a disobedient servant, an undutiful son, a brother who is one's enemy, he dares to set up a different altar against the bishops and priests of God whom he has treated despicably and has abandoned.

He dares to utter a different prayer in words that are not lawful, to desecrate the truth of the Lord's sacrifice by means of false offerings. Someone who strives against the official appointment of God is not the sort of person to grasp that he is punished by God's divine censure because of the outrageous character of his recklessness.[23]

---

[23]"Official appointment" = *ordinatio*, meaning "arrangement," or "formal disposition (of troops)," but which can also refer to the appointment of officials, and, indeed, ecclesiastically, to "ordination." We see here Cyprian combining a rhetoric of religious censure with that of political censure. Ps.-Hippolytus may have regarded Irenaeus' Church's offering (*Haer.* 4.17.4–18) as that of the bishop as Aaronic High Priest (*Trad. ap.* 3). Clement may have regarded στάσις as ἀνόσιος. But Cyprian goes further. Decius had come to the throne in an age of great political instability after wars with at least three other contenders. The persecution had been ended by the death of Decius and the succession of Trebonius Gallus. For Cyprian, in the light of such an experience, sacrilege (*profanare sacrificia*) and the defilement of the victim (*hostia*) on the altar (*altare*) were also political offences of a "rebel (*rebellis*)" against the *dispositio* or *ordinatio* of God, meriting punishment awarded following "judicial examination (*animaduersio*)" for one who has "committed treachery (*perfidus*)." He is helped by his OT exegesis in which worship and sacrifice outside of Jerusalem is contrary to the law of Deuteronomy. But his aim is to model the Church upon a kingdom and to incorporate into his description of church order secular Roman political concepts; see above n. 9 and Introduction §4.

18. Core, Dathan, and Abiron similarly revolted against God's priests.

Thus it was with Core, Dathan, and Abiron, who attempted to claim for themselves against Moses and Aaron the priest the privilege of offering sacrifice, and immediately paid the penalty for their attempts (Num 16.1–35). The earth gaped open into a deep cavity as its binding bonds burst asunder, whilst the gaping jaw produced by the receding soil swallowed up those who were standing and still alive. The wrath of the offended God struck not only those who were the instigators, but also fire, issuing from God, consumed with hastening retribution the two hundred and fifty remaining accomplices and camp followers of that violent madness.

These had gathered with these same men with the object of committing an outrage, thus of course clearly warning and revealing that the unprincipled would make any attempt by their human will to destroy God's officially appointed order. So also this happened in the case of king Ozias, when bearing the incense charger and violently taking possession for himself of the sacrifice contrary to God's law. Though Azarias the priest offered resistance, he was unwilling to comply and to give way (2 Kgs 26.16–20). Dismayed by God's wrath, he was also covered with the many spotted stains of leprosy on his brow, thus marked for having caused that offence to God on that part of his body where they are sealed who are obtaining God's merits.[24] And the sons of Aaron, who placed on the altar a strange fire that the Lord had not commanded, were wiped out immediately in the sight of the Lord in his vengeance (Lev 10.1–2).

19. Fallen but not schismatics can become martyrs through suffering.

These Old Testament examples are the models certainly followed by the schismatics. While disregarding God's tradition, they strive after alien doctrines and introduce the teachings of a human system.

---

[24]For the seal at baptism with the sign of the cross in oil, see n. 6 in Cyprian *Laps.* 2.

These are those whom the Lord reproaches and rebukes in his gospel, saying: "You have rejected the commandments of God so that you might establish your own tradition" (Mk 7.9).

Their indictment is worse than that to which the fallen lapsed are seen to have pleaded guilty. They are entreating God in order to make full amends in response to their guilty plea in the face of their indictment.[25] In their case the Church is sought and petitioned, but with the schismatics it is repudiated. The fallen were so under duress, but the latter committed a wicked, willful act. In the former case, the person has harmed only himself by his fall, but, in the latter, he has deceived the many whom he draws along with him by undertaking to embark on heresy or schism. In the former case, one person is penalized, but in the latter it is the many who are endangered.

The fallen Christian understands that the sin is of his own making, and he sorrows and beats his breast. The schismatic swells with pride in his fallen condition, and taking his pleasure in his own sins, he separates sons from their mother, he entices the sheep from their shepherd, he upsets solemn obligations to God. Though someone who has fallen has sinned once, the schismatic instead sins daily. Lastly, the fallen Christian, subsequently having obtained martyrdom, is able to take possession of the promises of the kingdom. The schismatic, if he were to be slain outside the Church, is unable to acquire the Church's rewards.

COMMENTARY CHAPTERS 20–24

Cyprian now addresses one of his major preoccupations, namely the authority traditionally accorded confessors and martyrs. He must refashion attitudes on this point. In some ways his words appear more applicable to the African confessors who had supported Felicissimus and the laxist party

[25]Here there is another rhetorical *tour de force* against the Novatianists, who condemned Cyprian for readmitting the fallen for the mortal sin of apostasy after penance. They are in a worse and not a better position before God than they might otherwise think.

rather than the Roman confessors who had sided with Novatian before returning to the Church. But the principle of the martyrs' authority that Cyprian attacked was central to his general approach to all groups, namely that only bishops duly ordained by other bishops, or priests whom they had ordained, could offer the Eucharist sacrifice and absolve. He would miss no opportunity to make this quite general point as he does now.

The confessors should not vaunt themselves against the priest of God. He also included references to fornication and adultery (20). But such general grounds for exclusion from the ranks of the confessors should not conceal from us those who are the real targets of Cyprian's attack. These were those confessors who sided with Novatian, and in their rigorism (rather than laxity) were guilty of "bad faith by leaving the Church . . . and rending asunder the its concord of unity" (21). Mentioning the example of Judas, he compares this with the followers of Novatian who were not true confessors, but were simply "joined in partnership with the confessors." He mentions those who distanced themselves "from the bad faith" of this group. We can identify these by name from other sources as Moyses, Nicostratus, and others who returned from Novatian's group. "They are as much to be praised for their preserving the peace of Christ as they were as victors in their conflict with the Devil" (22).

Cyprian now charges that true Christians must withdraw from the company of schismatics, in the light of God's command that the Church and the faith are one (23). They are assailing Christ's peace (24).

Text Chapters 20–24

20. Schismatics cannot appeal to the authority of the confessors.

It comes as no surprise, most beloved brethren, that even some of the confessors match some of those who also commit so heinous, so serious sins. After all, the office of confessor does not exempt anyone from the snares of the Devil. It does not guard some one still found in this world with everlasting protection against trials, perils and attacks by the secular authorities in the form of sudden outbursts of violence.

However, never before did we see amongst the confessors dishonest conduct as at present, as well as acts of fornication and of adultery, at which now, when we see it in certain of them, we express our sorrow and we grieve. Whoever a confessor might be, he is not greater nor better nor dearer to God than Solomon, who secured the grace which he sought from the Lord for as long as he walked in the ways of the Lord. After he forsook the way of the Lord, he also lost the grace of the Lord.

And for that reason it is written: "Hold fast that which you have lest another take it and receive your crown" (Rev 3.11) because, necessarily, the Lord would not threaten that the crown of righteousness could be taken away, unless it was because once righteousness had been withdrawn, it is necessary that also the crown should be withdrawn.

21. *The danger of confessorship leading to pride before a fall.*

The act of confessing Christ as the starting point in the race to glory is not already the successful end that merits the victor's garland. It does not mark the end of the act for which one wins praise, but makes a worthy beginning in that direction. Since it is written: "He who will persevere right up until the end, shall be saved" (Mt 24.13) whatever will be before that end is but a step by means of which one ascends to the summit of salvation, not the finishing post fixed at that summit's highest point.

He is a confessor: but after his act of confessing he is in greater peril since our adversary challenges him more. *He is a confessor*: he ought to agree more with the gospel of the Lord when he has obtained his glory from the Lord through his gospel. "To whom much is given, much is required of him" (Lk 12.48) and to whom more of value is credited, the greater the liability[26] that is exacted.

---

[26]"Liability" = *servitus*, otherwise translated "slavery" or "servitude." Once again Cyprian is using a legal concept, see Justinian (Ulpian) *Dig.* 8.2.1: "One of the owners of a house in common is not able to impose a liability (*servitutem*)."

No one should perish through a confessor's bad example, no one should learn injustice,[27] no one arrogance, no one bad faith from the conduct of a confessor.

He is a confessor: let him be humble and enjoy quietness, let him be moderate with discipline in his own public conduct, in order that he who is called a confessor of Christ might imitate the Christ whom he confesses. For Christ says: "He who exults himself shall be humbled, and he who humbles himself shall be exulted" (Lk 14.11). Christ himself has been exulted because, as the Word and Power and Wisdom of God the Father, he humbled himself on earth. Christ, who commanded humility, cannot love pride. He commanded humility to us according to his own law, and he himself received from the Father a far greater name as the reward for his humility (Phil 2.8–9).

He is a confessor of Christ: but not if afterward the majesty and dignity of Christ is blasphemed on his account. Let not the tongue that has confessed Christ be abusive, let it not be heard restless with passion, not resounding noisily with reproofs and lawsuits. Let it not strike against the brothers and priests of God with the poisonous words of the Serpent after his words of praise.[28] However, if he will later become deserving of censure and a subject of detestation, if he should fritter away his confession by bad association, if he should stain his life with shameful disgrace, he would end up changing his original act of faith by a later act of bad faith. This would be the consequence of leaving the Church where he was made a confessor. He cannot in that case delude himself with his confession as if he was chosen for the prize of glory when punishments that he merited were increasing further as a result of his own behavior in rending asunder the concord of the Church's unity.

[27]Once again Cyprian evaluates problems in the Church within the perspective of Roman political rhetoric. "Injustice (*iniustitia*)" describes upsetting a political order so that it is made chaotic, just as, from Cyprian's point of view, the Novatianists are upsetting divinely constituted church order.

[28]Is this a reference to sarcastically praising and condemning in forensic oratory? *Convicium* = "reproof," found in the sentence before, can mean "mockery."

22. The example of Judas shows that the majority can still stand firm.

Our Lord chose even Judas amongst the apostles, and, notwithstanding, Judas subsequently betrayed the Lord. But the validity and trust[29] of the apostles does not on this ground fail because Judas the betrayer departed from their association.

So also in this case. The sanctity and value of the confessors is not immediately diminished because the trust of some of them has been broken. The blessed Apostle speaks in his letter, in his own words: "For what if some of them have departed from the faith? Will ever their unbelief make God's trust empty? Far be it! For God is truthful, but every man false" (Rom 3.3–4). The greater and better part of the company of the confessors stands fast in the strength of their own faith, and in the truth of the Lord's law and discipline. People who are mindful of having obtained grace in the Church from the God who considered them worthy do not depart from the peace of the Church.

For this reason, in distancing themselves from the bad faith of those who were merely joined in partnership with the confessors, those who so separated themselves from such people have secured a far greater praise for their act of faith. They then withdrew from any taint of guilt. Enlightened truly with the lamp of the gospel, beaming with the pure and shining light of the Lord, they are as much to be praised for their preserving the peace of Christ as they were as victors in their conflict with the Devil.[30]

---

[29]"Validity and trust" = *firmitas et fides*, otherwise translated as "firmness and faith." I have translated them in what I believe to be Cyprian's legal context. For *firmitas* see Justinian (Ulpian) *Dig.* 24.1.13.1, where, on the question as to whether a husband's exile or divorce activates a wife's right to gifts willed by death: "His death must be awaited in order that his act might have full validity (*plenissimam habeat firmitatem*)." For *fides,* see Justinian (Ulpian) *Dig.* 40.5.37, where a freed slave is to: "render an account in good faith (*ex fide*)."

[30]This appears to be a reference to Moyses, Nicostratus, etc., who are mentioned in *Ep.* 27.4, 55.5.2, and in **Ep.*46.1, 51.1 and 54.4. They adhered initially to Novatian's party but subsequently "returned to the Church."

23. *Exhortation to unity.*

My desire as well as my exhortation and entreaty to you, therefore, most beloved brothers, is that if it can possibly be, none of the brothers may perish, and that our Mother might embrace joyfully within her bosom the one body of a people in agreement. If, however, our beneficial counsel is not able to recall to the way of salvation certain leaders of divisions and instigators of dissension, release the others from the snares of their deception. The leaders are likely to persist in their blind and stubborn madness. But we may release the remainder who are clearly under the sway of their simple natures, or lead on by their error, or deceived by some other crafty means of a deceptive trick.

Deliver their wandering footsteps from pathways in which they stray. Acknowledge the right path of the heavenly road. The Apostle voices his witness in agreement: "We instruct you," he says, "in the name of our Lord Jesus Christ, that you withdraw from all brothers who walk inordinately and not according to the tradition that they have received from us" (2 Thess 3.6) and again, he says: "Let no one deceive you with empty words: for on this account comes the wrath of God on the sons of willful disobedience. Be unwilling to be their partners" (Eph 5.6–7).

You must withdraw from wrong doers or at least avoid them. Someone who joins the company of those who walk badly and progress through the paths of error and guilt, wandering from the course of the true way, will himself be found guilty on the same charge.

God is one and Christ is one, and his Church and faith are one, and the people joined together with the glue of concord into the unbroken unity of a body. It is not possible for the unity to be rent asunder, nor the one body to be divided by the tearing apart of the structure, nor to be torn into fragments with the violent rending apart of its vital organs. Whatever splits off from the parent tree is not able to live and breathe apart from it. It loses the essential nature of health.[31]

[31]"Health" = *salus,* which also means salvation, and thus means the health of the tree or the salvation of a member of the body of Christ.

24. *Withdraw from the schismatics.*

The Spirit admonishes us with the words: "Who is the person who wishes for life and loves to see the best days? Hold back your tongue from evil and your lips that they speak not deceitfully. Turn from evil and do good, seek peace and follow her" (Ps 33.13–15). The son of peace ought to seek peace and pursue it. The person who recognizes and loves the bond of charity ought to hold in check his tongue from the evil of division.

Among his divine instructions and saving teachings, already near his Passion, the Lord said in addition: "Peace I leave with you, my peace I grant to you" (Jn 14.27). He gives us this inheritance, he promises all the gifts that he has pledged, and his rewards, on condition of the preservation of his peace. If we are the heirs of Christ, let us abide in Christ's peace. If we are the sons of God, we ought to be those who make peace. "Blessed," he says, "are the peacemakers since they themselves shall be called the sons of God" (Mt 5.9).

The sons of God ought to be peacemakers, gentle in heart, guileless in their speech, agreeing in purpose, holding together amongst themselves faithfully in the bonds of one mind.

COMMENTARY CHAPTERS 25–27

Cyprian now sets his doctrine of the unity of the Church into his general theory of historical decline that, as we saw in *Demetrian* 3–4, he shared with his pagan contemporaries. In the early Church of apostolic times, there was a joyful unity in which prayer was effective (25). But now, as the end of the age draws nigh, everything had declined into corruption of an original unity (26). Thus Cyprian concludes with the Scriptural exhortations of watching and waiting in preparation for the Lord's coming (27).

Text Chapters 25–27

25. The unity of the Early Church.

This one-mindedness once existed under the apostles. Thus the new people of faith, while guarding the commandments of God, held fast to his bond of love. The Scripture proves this with the words: "The crowd of those who believed however conducted themselves in one spirit and mind" (Acts 4.32) and again: "And they were all continuing in one mind in prayer with the women and Mary, who was the mother of Jesus, and with his brothers" (Acts 1.14). And in that spirit they prayed prayers that were efficacious, and in that spirit they were able to obtain with their faith whatever they were asking of God's mercy.

26. Diminution of this unity in recent times.

Amongst us indeed thus has this unity of heart and mind diminished, and so also the generosity of our religious service has been considerably lessened. They used once to sell houses and farms, and, laying up for themselves treasures in heaven, they offered the proceeds to the apostles for distribution to the poor. But now we neither give tithes from our paternal estate and, when the Lord orders us to sell, we prefer to buy and increase.

So the vitality of faith withers in us, so the strength of the believers droops, and for that reason the Lord, reviewing our time, says in his own gospel: "The Son of Man when he comes, do you think that he could find faith on earth?" (Lk 18.8)

We are seeing that what our Lord predicted is happening. There is not the confidence of faith in the fear of God, in the law of justice, in love, in good works. No one reflects on what is frightening about future events. No one considers the day of the Lord and the wrath of God, the punishments that will come upon those that believe not, and the eternal torments appointed for those who betray the faith. Whatever our conscience would fear if it believed in them, since it does not believe in them, our conscience does not fear anything at all. If however our conscience would believe in them, it would also take care. If our conscience took care, it might escape.

27. The Church must arise for the coming judgment.

Let us rouse ourselves as much as we are able, most beloved brothers, and, breaking short the sleep of the old sloth, let us keep awake for our observation and conduct of the precepts of the Lord. We are to be the kind of people that he himself instructed when he said: "May your loins be girded and your lamps burning, and, like those persons awaiting their Lord when he comes from the wedding so that, when he will come and knock, they shall open for him. Blessed are those servants whom the Lord arriving will find on watch" (Lk 12.35–37 and Mt 5.16). We ought to be girt lest, when the day of our being dispatched will come, it will catch us laden with baggage and otherwise involved in worldly affairs.

Let our light be resplendent in good works and may it shine, that the Lord himself may lead us from this world's night into the light of eternal brightness. Let us wait with expectation, always roused and on our guard for the sudden coming of the Lord so that, when he shall knock, our faith may be made awake, ready to receive the prize for our watchfulness from the Lord.

If we keep these commandments, if we hold fast to these admonitions and teachings, we will not be able to be overcome by our deceiving enemy while we are sleeping. We shall reign as servants on guard for Christ who exercises his Lordship over us.[32]

[32]For the eschatological dimension that Cyprian formally shares with his contemporaries, in which schismatics are symptomatic of the world's decline into chaos and disorder, see above n. 22.

Select Bibliography

Adolph, A., *Die Theologie der Einheit der Kirche bei Cyprian*, Europäische Hochschulstudien 33, 460 (Frankfurt am Main: Peter Lang, 1993).

Benko, S., "Pagan Criticisms of Christianity," in *Aufstieg und Niedergang der römischen Welt: Geschichte und Kultur Roms im Spiegel der neueren Forschung*, H. Temporini and W. Haase, eds. (Berlin and New York: De Gruyter Verlag, 1980), II.23.2, 1055–1118.

Benson, E. W., *Cyprian: His Life, His Times, His Work* (London: Macmillan, 1897).

Bévenot, M., *St Cyprian's De Unitate Chap. 4 in the Light of the MSS*, Analecta Gregoriana 11 (Rome, 1937).

————. "'Primatus Petro datur.' St Cyprian on the Papacy," *Journal of Theological Studies* 5 (1954): 19–35.

————. *The Tradition of Manuscripts: A Study in the Transmission of Cyprian's Treatises* (Oxford: Clarendon Press, 1961).

Bobertz, C. A., "The Historical Context of Cyprian's *De Unitate*," *Journal of Theological Studies* 42.1 (1990): 107–111.

————. "Patronal Letters of Commendation: Cyprian's *Epistulae* 38–40," *Studia Patristica* 24 (1991): 252–59.

————. "Patronage Networks and the Study of Ancient Christianity," *Studia Patristica* 24 (1991): 20–27.

————. "An Analysis of *Vita Cypriani* 3, 6–10 and the Attribution of *Ad Quirinum* to Cyprian of Carthage," *Vigiliae Christianae* 46 (1992): 112–28.

————. *Cyprian of Carthage as Patron: A Social and Historical Study of the Role of Bishop in the Ancient Christian Community of North Africa* (Ann Arbor: UMI, 1993).

Brent, A., *Cultural Episcopacy and Ecumenism: Representative Ministry in Church History from the Age of Ignatius of Antioch to the Reformation, with Special Reference to Contemporary Ecumenism*, Studies in Christian Mission 6 (Leiden: E. J. Brill, 1992).

————. "The Ignatian Epistles and the Threefold Ecclesiastical Order," *Journal of Religious History* 17.1 (1992): 18–32.

————. "Diogenes Laertius and the Apostolic Succession," *Journal of Ecclesiastical History* 44.3 (1993): 367–389.

————. *Hippolytus and the Roman Church in the Third Century: Communities in Tension before the Emergence of a Monarch-Bishop*, Supplements to *Vigiliae Christianae* 31 (Leiden: E.J. Brill, 1995).

————. *The Imperial Cult and the Development of Church Order: Concepts and Images of Authority in Paganism and Early Christianity before the Age of Cyprian*, Supplements to *Vigiliae Christianae* 45 (Leiden: E. J. Brill, 1999).

————. "Cyprian's Exegesis and Roman Political Rhetoric," in *L'Esegesi dei Padri Latini dale origini a Gregorio Magno*, in *Studia Ephemeridis Augustiniuanum* 68 (2000): 145–158.

————. "Cyprian and the Question of *ordinatio per confessionem*," *Studia Patristica* 36 (2001): 323–37.

————. "Cyprian's Reconstruction of the Martyr Tradition," *Journal of Ecclesiastical History* 53.2 (2002): 241–68.

Burns, J. Patout, "Social Context in the Controversy between Cyprian and Stephen," *Studia Patristica* 24 (1991): 38–44.

————. "On Rebaptism: Social Organization in the Third-Century Church," *Journal of Early Christian Studies* 1.4 (1993): 366–403.

————. "The Role of Social Structures in Cyprian's Response to the Decian Persecution," *Studia Patristica* 31 (1995): 260–67.

Clarke, G. W., "The Secular Profession of St Cyprian of Carthage," *Latomus* 24 (1965): 633–38.

————. "Some Observations on the Persecution of Decius," *Antichthon* 3 (1969): 63–76.

————. "The Epistles of Cyprian," in *Auckland Classical Essays Presented to E. M. Blaiklock*, ed. B. F. Harris, (Auckland: Auckland University Press; Wellington: Oxford University Press, 1970).

————. "Two Measures in the Persecution of Decius? Two Recent Views," *Bulletin of the Institute of Classical Studies* 20 (1973): 118–123.

————. "Double Trials in the Persecution of Decius," *Historia* 22 (1973): 650–63.

————. "Prosopographical Notes on the Epistles of Cyprian: III. Rome in August 258," *Latomus* 34.2 (1975): 437–48.

————. *The Letters of St Cyprian*, 4 vols, Ancient Christian Writers, 43, 44, 46 and 47 (New York: Newman Press 1984, 1986, and 1989).

De Ste. Croix, G. E. M., "Why were the Early Christians Persecuted?—A Rejoinder," *Past and Present* 27 (1964): 28–33.

Dunn, G., "Infected Sheep and Diseased Cattle, or the Pure and Holy Flock: Cyprian's Pastoral Care of Virgins," *Journal of Early Christian Studies* 11.1 (2003): 1–20.

Fahey, M. A., *Cyprian and the Bible: A Study in Third-Century Exegesis*, Beiträge zur Geschichte der Biblischen Hermeneutik 9 (Tübingen: Mohr-Siebeck, 1971). [Augustin. P323.2]

Fitzgerald, P. J., "A Model For Dialogue: Cyprian Of Carthage On Ecclesial Discernment," *Theological Studies* 59.2 (1998): 236–253.

Frend, W. C. H., *Martyrdom and Persecution in the Early Church* (Oxford: Blackwell, 1965).

Hein, K., *Eucharist and Excommunication: A Study in Early Christian Doctrine and Discipline* (Frankfurt: Herbert and Peter Lang, 1973).

Janssen, L. F., "'Superstitio' and the Persecution of the Christians," *Vigiliae Christianae* 33.2 (1979): 131–59.

Justinian, *Digest*, edited by T. Mommsen and P. Krueger, with an English Translation by A. Watson (Philadelphia: University of Pennsylvania Press, 1985).

Keresztes, P., "The Decian Libelli and Contemporary Literature," *Latomus* 34.3 (1975): 761–81.

————. "Two Edicts of the Emperor Valerian," *Vigiliae Christianae* 29 (1975): 81–95.

Knipfing, J. R., "The Libelli of the Decian Persecution," *Harvard Theological Review* 16 (1923): 345–390.

Lampe, G. W. H., *The Seal of the Spirit: A Study in the Doctrine of Baptism and Confirmation in the New Testament and the Fathers* (London: SPCK, 1967).

Laurance, J. D., *The Priest as Type of Christ: The Leader of the Eucharist in Salvation History according to Cyprian of Carthage*, American University Studies 7.5 (New York: Peter Lang, 1984).

————. "'There Is but One Baptism in the Holy Church': A Theological Appraisal of the Baptismal Controversy in the Work and Writings of Cyprian of Carthage," *Theological Studies* 59.4 (1998): 763–63.

Leppin, V., "Reinstating Episcopal Representation after Christian Persecution according to Cyprian of Carthage—Developing a Theology of Church Unity," *Zeitschrift für Antikes Christentum* 4.2 (2000): 255–69.

Moorhead, J., "Papa as 'Bishop of Rome,'" *Journal of Ecclesiastical History* 36.3 (1985): 337–50.

Musurillo, H., *Acts of the Christian Martyrs. Introduction. Texts and Translations* (Oxford: Clarendon Press, 1972).

Osborn, E. F., "Cyprian's Imagery," *Antichthon* 7 (1973): 65–79.

Rives, J. B., *Religion and Authority in Roman Carthage from Augustus to Constantine* (Oxford: Clarendon Press, 1995).

Sage, M. M., *Cyprian*, Patristics Monographs Series 1 (Philadelphia Patristic Foundation: Philadelphia, 1975).

Scott, J., "Saint Cyprian's Episcopal Letters," *Journal of Theological Studies* 52.1 (2001): 359–61.

Stewart–Sykes, A., "Ordination Rites and Patronage Systems in Third-Century North Africa," *Vigiliae Christianae* 56.2 (2002): 115–30.

Torrance, I., "They Speak to Us across the Centuries. 2. Cyprian," *Expository Times* 108.12 (1997): 356–59.

Walker, G. S. M., "The Churchmanship of St Cyprian," *Ecumenical Studies in History* 9 (London: Lutterworth, 1968).

Ward Perkins, J. B. and Goodchild, R. G., "The Christian Antiquities of Tripoli Tania," in *Archaeologia* 45 (1953): 1–84.

POPULAR PATRISTICS SERIES

ST VLADIMIR'S SEMINARY PRESS
1-800-204-2665 • www.svspress.com